A Year of Women's Programs

by V. Louise
Cunningham

 STANDARD PUBLISHING
Cincinnati, Ohio   2972

To
Downey, his patience, love and understanding about the paper chaos and Mary Lou who critiqued and encouraged me.

Illustrated by Romilda Dilley

Cover photo by Robert C. Hayes

Unless otherwise noted, all Scripture quotations are from the *Holy Bible, New International Version.* Copyright ©1978 International Bible Society. Used by permission of Zondervan Bible Publishers.

Library of Congress Cataloging-in-Publication Data

Cunningham, V. Louise (Verna Louise), 1933-
   Change me, Lord

    1. Church work with women. 2. Women—Religious life. I. Title.
BV4445.C86   1988   259'.088042   87-18110
ISBN 0-87403-356-X

Copyright ©1988. The STANDARD PUBLISHING Company.
Cincinnati, Ohio.
Division of STANDEX INTERNATIONAL Corporation.
Printed in U.S.A.

CONTENTS

Program		Page
1	Change Me	5
2	Changed by Storms	13
3	Changed by Thanking	19
4	Changed by God's Gift	25
5	Changed by Bible Study	31
6	Changed by Love	37
7	Changed by Prayer	43
8	Changed Appearance	50
9	Changed by Serving	59
10	Changed by Trusting	66
11	Changed by Obedience	72
12	Changed by Praising	77

PREFACE

This series of women's programs, *Change Me, Lord,* will help your group of ladies grow in their Christian faith and their relationship with God. Writing in their prayer journals is an important part of these programs. In this way they are able to apply what they learn to their daily lives.

The short dramatic skits are easily done with a minimum of staging, memory work, or acting ability. Provision has been made so notes may be easily used. A number of ladies may be involved in each program.

An example for a name tag has been included in each program. Use these for members and guests so all will feel welcome. Suggestions for decorations, refreshments, and songs are given for each program. However, any of these may be changed or adapted to meet the needs of your group.

A short poem relative to the program has been included in each program. The poem may be read by one of the ladies during the program, given out as a handout, or used as part of the room decorations.

Enjoy the programs and be prepared for some changes within your group.

1 Thessalonians 5:18

Program 1

Change Me

Name Tag

Program Outline

                Song: "Turn Your Eyes Upon Jesus"
          Scripture: Ruth 1
            Prayer
Program Feature: Thoughts from book of Ruth, talk show with guest stars, Ruth and Naomi
        Discussion
  Taking Action: Start a spiritual journal
            Prayer
              Song: "Where He Leads I'll Follow"
    Decorations: Happy faces
  Refreshments: Cookies or cupcakes with happy faces.

Name Tags may be made using the sample provided here. Be sure to introduce guests and make sure they are included in all activities.

Decorations: Decorate by placing cutouts of happy faces around the room.

Refreshments: Cupcakes, cookies, or a large cake decorated with happy faces and usual beverages.

Song: "Turn Your Eyes Upon Jesus" (also titled "The Heavenly Vision")

Scripture: Ruth 1

Prayer: Dear Heavenly Father, we pray that our hearts will be open to see the areas we can change in our lives, that we who live in seemingly impossible situations will turn our hearts from bitterness. Help us to realize we can control our actions and reactions. Help us to change to be the person we can become. We pray in Jesus' name, Who gives us wisdom and power when we ask, amen.

Program Feature

(Leader brings in a thermometer, holds it up and explains.) When a thermometer is exposed to cold, the mercury in it goes down. When heat is applied, the mercury rises. We don't have to be like a thermometer. We can change our lives by not reacting to our surroundings.

We are going to look briefly at the lives of three women who had choices to make. These choices changed their lives. Did these women react to their circumstances like thermometers or could they have changed their attitudes?

Naomi, Elimelech and their two sons, Mahlon and Kilion, left Bethlehem because of a severe famine and moved to Moab, a country east of the Dead Sea.

Elimelech died leaving Naomi and her two sons. The sons married women of Moab even though law-abiding Israelites were forbidden to do so. The two sons died. In ten years,

Naomi had lost her husband and her sons. Naomi was desolate. She had not adjusted to a foreign country and its worship of idols, so when she heard things were better in Bethlehem, she decided to return to her homeland. Her daughters-in-law, Ruth and Orpah, started out with her.

(Leader is interrupted by a woman who gives her a note. Leader silently reads the note and turns to the group.) We are fortunate. There is a talk show on TV that fits right in with our lesson. Let's watch it.

SKIT

(Hostess of the talk show is behind a desk or a little bit apart from the other two women. Hostess is interviewing Naomi and Ruth. All the women can have notes in front of them.)

Hostess: Ruth and Naomi, I know this is your first appearance on a talk show and you may be nervous, so feel free to refer to any notes you might have brought with you. Ruth, as I understand it, you are to be married to Boaz very soon. Since you are from Moab, how did you meet him?

Ruth: After we arrived in town, Naomi told me to go and glean in his field.

Hostess: Maybe we should ask Naomi how she met you.

Naomi: My husband Elimelech, our two sons, Mahlon and Kilion, and I went to Moab during a famine. Elimelech died and I was left with our two sons. They married Moabite girls, Orpah and Ruth. We lived there about ten years. *(Sadly.)* It's all a nightmare. *(Pause.)* Both my sons died and there we were, three widows.

Hostess: That must have been very difficult for you to be a widow in a foreign country.

Naomi: What bothered me the most was that the Moabites worshiped idols. Elimelech and I tried to keep our belief strong in a foreign culture, but it was difficult.

Hostess: Ruth, what did you think about these people who came to your country believing in a different god than you were accustomed to?

Ruth: We believed each country had its own gods, and it was difficult to understand a God who was over all nations and people. I think I was drawn to Naomi and Elimelech by their faith and homelife. I wanted to learn more about their God.

Hostess: Is that why you decided to come back with Naomi?

Ruth: Yes.

Hostess: As I understand it, Orpah didn't come all the way with you. What happened?

Naomi: When I heard the famine was over, I wanted to come back to my people. We all packed up and started on our way.

Ruth: We had traveled a short distance and Naomi told us to go back to our mother's home. She gave us this blessing. "May the Lord grant that each of you will find rest in the home of another husband" (Ruth 1:9). She kissed us and we all cried. We both insisted we would go with her to her people.

Naomi: I couldn't understand why they would come with me. I couldn't have any more children. I felt the Lord's hand was against me. *(Dabs at eyes with handkerchief.)* Orpah cried and kissed me and turned back. Ruth wouldn't let go of my hand. I'll never forget her words. She said, "Don't urge me to leave you or to turn back from you. Where you go I will go, and where you stay I will stay. Your people will be my people and your God my God" (Ruth 1:16).

Ruth: I finally convinced her she couldn't leave me behind.

Hostess: Naomi, when you arrived in Bethlehem you asked people to call you Mara, which means bitter. Is that correct?

Naomi: Yes. I felt the Almighty had brought nothing but misfortune on me. I had gone away full but the Lord brought me back empty.

Hostess: Here we have three women and three choices. Orpah made the choice to stay in her homeland. We don't know if she was frightened of the unknown or would rather have a god who didn't speak or act. From what Ruth told me earlier today, she hasn't heard from Orpah to know if she's sorry she didn't come with them. Ruth, tell us a little more about yourself. Your choice was to come with Naomi. What led to that choice? How did you feel?

Ruth: My first big choice had been to marry an Israelite. There was a certain amount of loyalty to Naomi to make the choice to go with her. I knew it would be difficult to come into a foreign culture and I wondered if I would be accepted.

Since it is the custom to leave the leftover grain in the fields for the poor, I went to glean. Later I found it was the field belonging to Boaz. He's from the same clan as my father-in-law, Elimelech. Boaz noticed me and was very kind from the first. I continued to work in his fields. Now I am to marry him, and I'm very happy.

Hostess: I can tell you are a very happy lady and will make a beautiful bride. Now, let's get back to you, Naomi. I've had some difficult things happen in my life, although not as serious as yours. You asked to be called Mara meaning bitter when you came back to Bethlehem. Do you think a person can choose to be bitter or sad in her circumstances? In thinking back on those days in Moab, is there anything you could have done to change your attitude?

Naomi: I'm not sure I know what you mean by having a choice in my attitude.

Hostess: I believe we have control over our attitudes. We can choose to be happy or sad. I'd like to ask our studio audience about their feelings on this subject and if they have any questions to ask the ladies?

Leader: Excuse me, but I'd like to say this before we open up to questions, if I may?

(Hostess nods agreement.)

Leader: People read the book of Ruth and figure Naomi was full of self-pity and bitterness. Let's take into consideration, when we talk to her, that she didn't know all the things we know today. We believers in the living Lord have the Holy Spirit dwelling within us to help us through our daily trials. Naomi didn't. We have the advantage of the New Testament which is the inspired words of God. Naomi couldn't put words like "Give thanks in all circumstances" (1 Thessalonians 5:18) on her refrigerator as a reminder. History can't be repeated, but could Naomi have chosen a different attitude? What can we say that may have helped her?

Discussion

Possible Questions
1. Do you think that Elimelech and Naomi leaving Bethlehem showed a lack of faith in God's providing for them during the famine?
2. Naomi must have been a good mother-in-law for Ruth to want to go with her to Bethlehem. What do you think Ruth saw in her, or did she go because of pity, loyalty, gratitude, or to learn about God?
3. What about our behavior, moods, feelings, and temperaments? Are they results of how we think? What do others see?
4. If someone in our family wakes up in a bad mood, does it influence our whole day?
5. If we live with an alcohol-or drug-dependent person, can we change our attitude?
6. If one is a widow like Naomi, can one change her attitude toward God and life?
7. If someone hurts us, do we chew on that thought all day long like a dog worrying a bone? Do we tell everyone all about it? What else could we do? *(Take it to the Lord in prayer. Pray for that person. Have a forgiving, understanding spirit so we will not grow resentful.)*

Leader: Paul made a choice. He wrote this after receiving a gift. Let's read Philippians 4:11, 12.

"I am not saying this because I am in need, for I have learned to be content whatever the circumstances. I know what it is to be in need, and I know what it is to have plenty. I have learned the secret of being content in any and every situation."

Paul knew how to be content, whether he was hungry or in prison. He learned to be content in every situation. He had decided what his attitude would be.

Our way of thinking is our most difficult problem. The way we think about ourselves, others, and events around us will decide what kind of person we are and how we will react. Our thinking patterns influence our behavior. God has a plan and a purpose.

Paul went through many traumatic experiences, but yet he wrote of joy and rejoicing. He had learned to be content with or without many comforts.

Job is another person who went through many trials. Job spoke about gold. He wrote, "But he knows the way that I take; when he has tested me, I will come forth as gold" (Job 23:10). To burn off the impurities, the old-time goldsmith heated gold with intense heat. These impurities rose to the surface and were skimmed off. When the goldsmith could see his face in the gold, he knew it was pure.

God is our goldsmith. Many of us are even now being tested so we can come forth as gold. He allows us to undergo trials to remove our impurities like obstinacy, lack of faith, lack of concern and compassion, self-centeredness, self-pity, or self-righteousness so we can reflect Christ in our lives. We can change ourselves and our attitudes.

(Hold up thermometer.) We don't have to react to things in our lives the way this thermometer does. Sometimes our changing is threatening and things could get worse when we don't react the way we normally do. When we have a better attitude, our situation will improve.

Change Me

A thermometer records the temperature.
   It soars or falls with the weather.
   All the world can change it.

Am I a thermometer of my world?
   If I seesaw in my moods,
   I've let the world change me.

When I reject resentment, fear, and hate,
   And spread God's love.
   I've let God change me.

I can be patient, loving, and kind;
   Choose to be happy or sad
   When I let Him change me.

The decision is mine to follow God's way.
   I want to be His instrument,
   And let my Lord change me.

Taking Action: As an aid in changing our attitudes, we will each keep a spiritual journal this year. Each day take a few minutes and write a letter to God. This is for you, not for sharing. Bare your emotions. How you feel and think. This is not a diary of what you did, but how you felt. How did you react? How did you feel about this? Get to know yourself through this tool. Then you can be excited about seeing how you are growing spiritually. Watch changes take place in your attitude.

This month, write down in particular how you could have made a better choice. This is not to chastise yourself but to learn, "I can make a choice in my attitude."

Prayer: Dear Heavenly Father, thank You for loving and accepting us as we are. May we learn how to handle our actions and reactions when life's experiences wear us down. Help us to recognize with Your strength, we can make the changes in ourselves we need to make. Help us remember we have a choice as to what kind of attitude we will have. In Jesus' name, we pray, amen.

Song: "Where He Leads I'll Follow"

Refreshments: Encourage refreshment time to be a fun time of fellowship.

Program 2

Changed by Storms

Name Tag

Program Outline

Song: "Jesus Calls Us"
Scripture: Mark 4:35-41
Prayer
Program Feature: Introduction
Discussion: Lifeboat Drill
Taking Action: Continue with journals
Prayer
Song: "He Is Able to Deliver Thee"
Decorations: Verses on life preservers
Refreshments: Donuts and hot-spiced cider

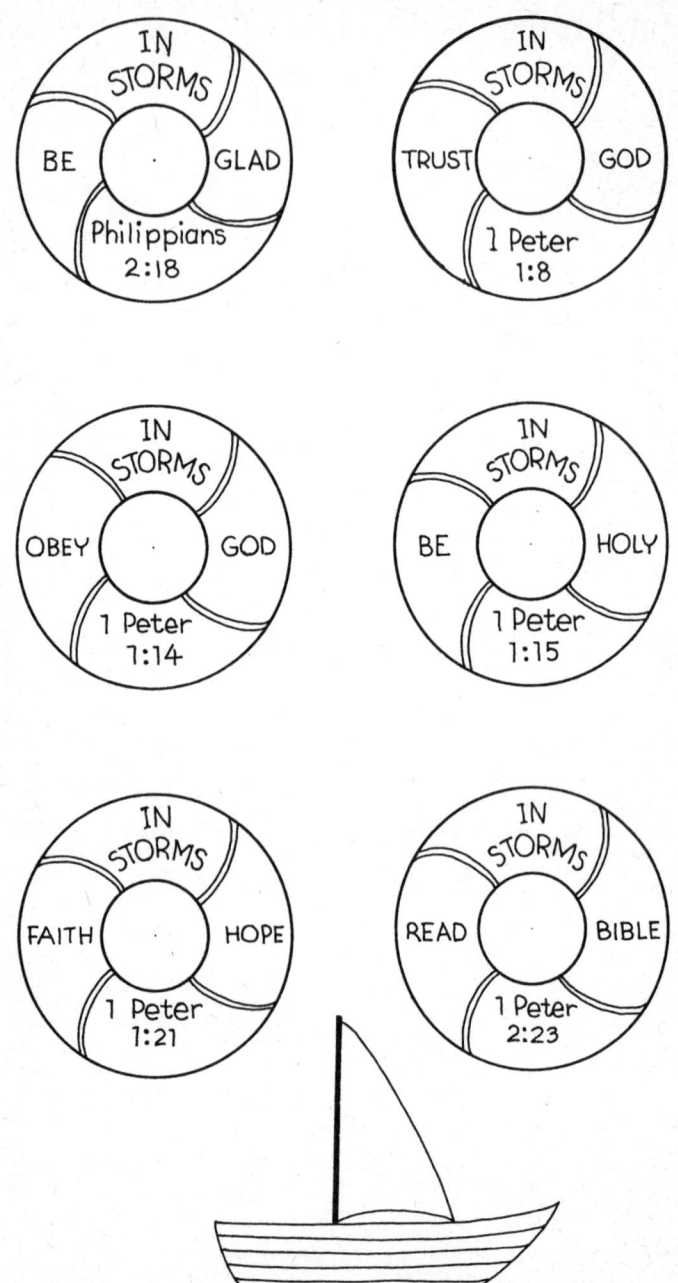

Name Tags may be made using the sample here. Be sure to introduce guests and make sure they are included in all activities.

Decorations: Pictures of boats placed around the room, six life preservers drawn like these samples using the suggested Scriptures.

Refreshments: Donuts and hot-spiced cider. Decorate the donuts so they resemble life preservers.

Song: "Jesus Calls Us"

Scripture: Mark 4:35-41

Prayer: Oh, Lord, we read how the disciples had the physical presence of Jesus in their fishing boat, yet they were afraid. Sometimes it is hard for us to trust You, Father, during the storms of our lives. Help us not to panic when the waves grow high and the wind blows our spiritual boats around. Remind us Jesus is in our boats and You are in control. We pray in His name, amen.

Leader: It was a normal boat ride for the disciples until the storm came up. The waves broke over the boat and it was nearly swamped, so even the hardy fishermen felt overwhelmed by the storm. Jesus was in the stern, sleeping on a cushion, yet the disciples were afraid even though they had the physical presence of Jesus with them.

What about us? Let's think of our lives as being in a spiritual boat and, as believers, we have Jesus with us. We sail along on the sea of life and the ocean is calm and the sun is shining. Then problems confront us and we get seasick. There are other times when our boat is becalmed, and instead of waiting for the wind, we row or start an auxiliary motor. We feel better with noise and motion even though they take us in the wrong direction.

We enter a time of storm in our lives. Dark clouds hover above our boat. Lightning flashes fitfully across the horizon and thunder bellows in a loud voice. The rain bombards us. The wind piles up the waves like mountains and our boat tosses. The masts creak and groan, rain pelts down on us, and our faces are white with fear.

We bring on some storms in our lives by our own actions, and other times the rough waters are brought into our lives by someone else's boat. Their wake swamps our little boat. Some of the storms we have are caused because of lashing our boat with another person's boat. This happens in marriage or business. If we fight for control, we paddle in different directions, and we may end up on the rocks. We need to agree on how to handle the boat and where we are headed. When rough waters are brought into our lives we need to remember we do not have control over another person's boat, but we do have control over our own boat.

As our boat bobs up and down, we see friends who don't have a storm around them, and we wonder why their lives are so smooth and why this happened to us. Self-pity or wishful thinking will make us uncomfortable and sink our boat because our selfish nature tends to focus on what is missing from our lives rather than the challenges and opportunities we have. We don't want to ignore problems but recognize life involves good and bad, happiness and sorrow, contentment and frustration.

We can't stop the wind and waves. We leave the sail up and fight the storm in our way. We are afraid we'll sink and drown but are too proud to ask for help. We don't want to be totally dependent on God. We feel we can take over the tiller and we end up crosswise of the waves and they wash over us. We need to let God have control.

Let's see what God is doing in our storms and the provisions He has given us by having a lifeboat drill.

Discussion

Lifeboat Drill: *(Divide the ladies into small groups. Give each leader a list of Scriptures and have the groups discuss the following questions. If time is short, divide up the questions. One person from each group will report to the entire group what each group has learned.)*

Questions and Scripture to be Handed Out
1. What difference does God's being omnipresent make in your storm? Does this comfort you?
   Scriptures: Isaiah 43:1; Psalm 139

2. How can we be changed by storms?
   Scriptures: Romans 5:3-5; James 1:2-4; Job 23:10; 1 Peter 1:6, 7
3. How does God use the storms in our lives for His honor and glory?
   Scriptures: Romans 8:28, 29; John 9:1-3
4. What are the rewards or benefits of storms?
   Scriptures: 2 Corinthians 4:17; Galatians 6:9; 2 Corinthians 1:3, 4; 2 Corinthians 12:7-10; 1 Peter 2:12; 3:13, 14

(After the allotted time, reassemble back in the large group. The ladies will share what they have learned. Following the question is a summary that can be used in addition to other points the ladies have mentioned.)

Question 1—We were to see what difference God's being omnipresent has made in our lives. We have learned that God is always with us, always within reach so He can comfort us.

God knows our individual situations. He has a plan. He allows problems into our lives not by chance or accident. These storms come with His knowledge, not to hurt us but to help us develop into the more Christlike person God wants us to be. Our storms and our response to those storms should glorify God.

God loves us and His love is like a life preserver—it surrounds us. God is mightier than the storm.

Question 2—How can we be changed by storms? In Romans 5 and James 1 we learned that storms build our characters. In Job 23 and 1 Peter 1 we found that storms refine us like gold.

Question 3—Romans 8 and John 9 teach us that God can use everything in our lives for His honor and glory.

Question 4—What are the rewards? The rewards or benefits are varied. Our storms are achieving for us an eternal glory (2 Corinthians 4:17). We will reap a harvest (Galatians 6:9). They will make us sympathetic (2 Corinthians 1:3, 4). Storms will humble us (2 Corinthians 12:7-10), and how we handle our storms will be a witness (I Peter 2:12). We want our witness to be a good witness.

Today we have looked at many Scriptures that will encourage us in stormy weather. We need to realize that no one else can make us happy or meet all our needs. Our deepest longing can't be satisfied by marriage, family, friends, or work. It is difficult, but when we focus on the needs of others and help them bail out their boat, our own boat becomes less water-filled.

We can read our book of instructions, the Bible, and make sure Jesus is in our boat. He only comes by invitation and won't take control of our ship's wheel unless we allow Him. Trust Him. He won't wreck our keel but will help us through the storm and into a safe harbor. Our relationship with God is the most important thing. It's been said, God calms the storm or calms His child.

Taking Action: Hasn't writing in your spiritual journal every day been very helpful for you this past month? I want to encourage you to continue writing every day because it will help you to see the changes taking place in your life. This month we want to concentrate on one storm in our lives. We'll write about it in our journal, and reread the Scriptures we read today. Try to see God's perspective in your storm.

Prayer: Dear Heavenly Father, You are aware of the storms in each of our lives. Help us to turn over control of our little spiritual boat to You, trusting You to bring us safely through the storms. We thank You for loving us so much and being with us at all times. Help us to concentrate on the wonder and delight of You and Your perspective. We thank and praise You. In Jesus' name, amen.

Song: "He Is Able to Deliver Thee"

Refreshments: Use this time for fellowship.

Captain

The billows crash, the wind blows strong.
My little skiff is tossed about,
But God is ruler of the sea.

My ship is assailed on every side.
He guides my ship through waters deep,
Since God is captain of my skiff.

In darkest night, He lights my way.
I feel His presence always near,
Since God is captain of my soul.

Program 3

Changed by Thanking

Name Tag

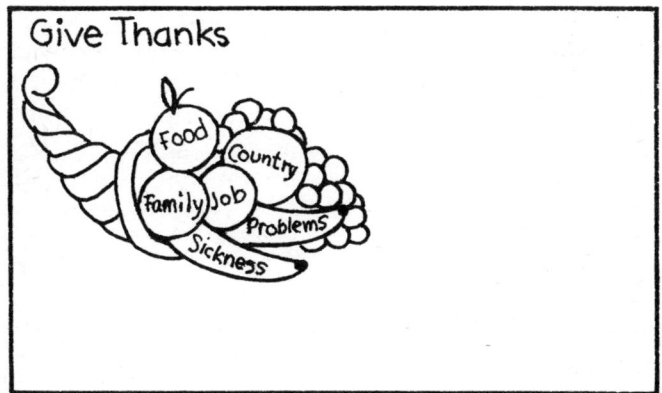

Program Outline

Song:	"We Gather Together"
Scripture:	1 Thessalonians 5:18
Prayer	
Program Feature:	Skit based on 1 Thessalonians 5:18
Discussion	
Taking Action:	Each day, write in journal three things for which you are thankful.
Prayer	
Song:	"Come, Ye Thankful People, Come"
Refreshments:	Pumpkin pie, pumpkin bread, or pumpkin cookies
Decorations:	Fall flowers, cornucopia, gourds, or other fall arrangements

Name Tags may be made using the sample here. Be sure to introduce guests and help them feel welcome.

Decorations: Use Indian corn, gourds, basket of apples, or fall flower arrangement. Posters using the design on page 4 may be placed around the room.

Refreshments: Pumpkin pie, pumpkin bread, or pumpkin cookies and favorite beverages.

Song: "We Gather Together"

Scripture: 1 Thessalonians 5:18

Prayer: Dear Heavenly Father, help us to realize how many things we have in our lives for which we can give You our thanks and praise. We pray that our time together will fill each of our hearts with thanksgiving and appreciation for all You are doing in our lives. We commit this time for Your honor and glory. In Jesus' name we pray, amen.

Program Feature   SKIT

Scene: *(Four ladies—Leader, Natalie, Joan, and Colleen—are gathered around a table to plan a Thanksgiving meeting. The ladies don't have to memorize all their lines, they can refer to papers on the table.)*

Leader: We need to plan our meeting for November. The theme for our program is Thanksgiving.
Natalie: What else? It's November.
Joan: I think it will be difficult for many of our ladies to be thankful this year because their husbands can't find work.
Colleen: Give thanks in all circumstances.
Leader: We also have some new widows in our congregation. They may not be feeling very thankful either. We need to have a program that will help them.
Colleen: Give thanks in all circumstances.
Natalie: My problems aren't very serious, but a lot of the time I find it hard to be thankful. Colleen, why do you always say "Give thanks in all circumstances"? Is it in the Bible?

Leader: That verse is 1 Thessalonians 5 something, isn't it?
Colleen: 1 Thessalonians 5:18. "Give thanks in all circumstances, for this is God's will for you in Christ Jesus." This verse explains why we should give thanks.
Leader: It says to give thanks *IN* not *FOR* all circumstances.
Natalie: I don't understand.
Colleen: God didn't say to give thanks in all circumstances *except* for loss of a job or give thanks in all circumstances *except* in the death of a loved one, or give thanks in all circumstances *except* sickness. God didn't make any exceptions.
Joan: True, but how can we explain to others, and even ourselves, who have such problems, that we can have thankful hearts?
Natalie: How is that practical for today?
Leader: Maybe that is the way we should approach the subject. How can we have thankful hearts in every circumstance?
Natalie: If you can convince me, maybe you can convince others.
Colleen: What is the best way to help the ladies really believe this?
Joan: We could talk about things that keep us from having thankful hearts, like pride.
Colleen: We could point out all the Scripture verses that tell us to be thankful. God said it often, so He knows we can.
Leader: Just quoting Bible verses that say to be thankful may not be that helpful unless we give the ladies a list of some of the verses. They could look the Scripture up during their prayer times and use them as a guide. But we need to give the ladies more.
Joan: That's a good idea.
Natalie: I don't know. Do you think the ladies would look the Scriptures up?
Leader: When they realize the Scriptures are helpful to their understanding, they will look them up. Let's go back to what Joan said. What keeps us from having thankful hearts? She said pride.
Colleen: When we have a prideful spirit, we think we are always right. This makes us hard to live or work with. Pride can make us defensive and impatient.

Joan: We tend to hold grudges and have a critical attitude when we are full of pride.

Leader: Worry is another reason that keeps us from being thankful. Some people call it being *burdened* or *concerned,* but worry is wrong.

Colleen: Some people complain about what they don't have instead of being thankful for what they do have.

Natalie: That's a good point. We can concentrate on what we have rather than on what we don't have.

Leader: Discouragement is contagious. Worry and pride keep us from having thankful hearts. Then what do you suggest we do?

Colleen: If we thank and praise God, our attitude will change.

Joan: Praise shows we are trusting God and walking by faith, not sight. If we don't have a thankful attitude, we are saying God doesn't know what He is doing.

Leader: Thanksgiving becomes a way of life.

Colleen: It's been said, thanksgiving or thanksliving.

Natalie: But sometimes I don't feel thankful. What do I do then?

Leader: The change doesn't happen overnight, but God will help us give thanks since it is an act of our will, not an emotion. God will release His power in our lives if we ask Him.

Joan: That's very true. If we are thankful to God for our circumstances, they may not go away; but He will give us the strength to cope with the problem and praise Him in all circumstances.

Colleen: We need to point out that thanking and praising God is different than being content in accepting our circumstances. God expects us to change the things in our circumstances that we can change and to accept the things we can't change. We need to get excited about what is happening and express complete approval that God is doing what is best for us. He allows us to be where we are for a reason. We don't always know and understand, but we don't have to. We can rely on knowing God wants what is best for us.

Leader: There is the verse that says, "Rejoice in the Lord always. I will say it again: Rejoice!" (Philippians 4:4). It says to rejoice, not to be content. Rejoicing is being glad, showing great pleasure or being delighted.

Natalie: So what you are saying is this: we will not have a problem-free life, but if we have a thankful heart, God will give us the faith and inner resources to rise above the problems.

Joan: We could open the meeting for questions and ask some of the women what has worked for them. That should encourage others.

Leader: It would also be a good idea to take time and let each lady list the things she can thank God for. Well, ladies, I think we will have a good program. Shall we adjourn our meeting?

Program Leader: That was a great idea they presented. At this time we will hand out a list of Scripture verses that you may use as a reference during your prayer times. Turn the paper over and on the back, start a list of things for which you are thankful, including circumstances you are *in* at this time.

Verses of Thanks and Praise

Let them give thanks to the Lord for his unfailing love and his wonderful deeds for men. Let them sacrifice thank offerings and tell of his works with songs of joy (Psalms 107:21, 22).

At midnight I rise to give you thanks for your righteous laws (Psalm 119:62).

Speak to one another with psalms, hymns and spiritual songs. Sing and make music in your heart to the Lord, always giving thanks to God the Father for everything, in the name of our Lord Jesus Christ (Ephesians 5:19, 20).

Let the peace of Christ rule in your hearts, since as members of one body you were called to peace. And be thankful (Colossians 3:15).

It is good to praise the Lord and make music to your name, O Most High (Psalm 92:1).

Enter his gates with thanksgiving and his courts with praise; give thanks to him and praise his name (Psalm 100:4).

When you have eaten and are satisfied, praise the Lord (Deuteronomy 8:10).

Others: Psalm 68:19; Acts 28:15; 2 Corinthians 9:15; 1 Timothy 1:12; 1 Corinthians 15:57

Discussion: Ask ladies to share part of their list of the things they are thankful for.

Taking Action: By your journal entries, are you beginning to see the changes taking place? When you wrote about the storms in your life this past month, did it change how you felt about your storm?

Each day this month write in your journal three things for which you are thankful, such as a plant blooming which brings pleasure or a phone call from a friend. They don't have to be big things.

Prayer: Oh, Lord, You in Your wisdom know the set of circumstances we are in. You have such love for us and know what is best. You can see the whole picture of our lives and know what kind of women we can become. Help us not only to be thankful but to go the next step and praise You. Help us have the assurance You will work all things for good as we grow more and learn to obey and trust You more. In Jesus' name, amen.

Song: "Come, Ye Thankful People, Come"

Refreshments: Enjoy this time of sharing together.

Thanks

Thanks for the teardrops of dew on the rose.
Thanks for the sunbeams between the clouds.
Thanks for the birds that sing in the rain.

Thanks for wisdom beyond understanding.
Thanks for the way you've chosen for me.
Thanks for Who You are, my Lord and King.

Program 4

Changed by God's Gift

Name Tag

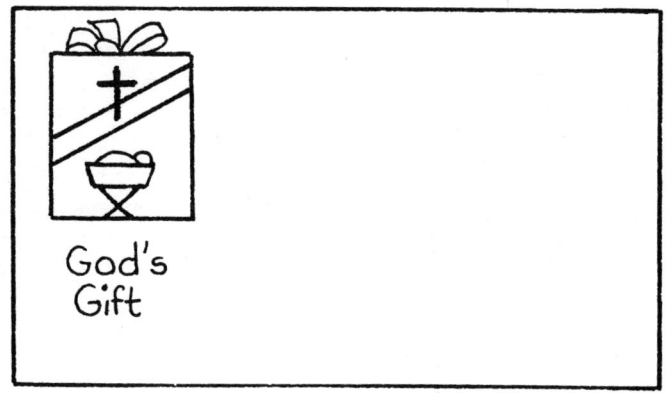

Program Outline

          Song: "Joy to the World!"
         Prayer
     Scripture: Luke 2:1-20
          Song: "What Child Is This?"
       Reading: "Heaven Touched Earth"
          Song: "Thou Didst Leave Thy Throne"
       Reading: "Perfect Gift"
          Song: "Silent Night"
    Meditation: Changed by God's Gift
  Taking Action
         Prayer
          Song: "O Come, All Ye Faithful"
   Refreshments: Christmas cookies or breads
    Decorations: Candle and evergreen branches

Name Tags may be made using the sample provided here. Introduce guests and include them in all activities.

Decorations: Place candles and evergreen branches on the tables. Wrapped gift boxes may be placed around the room.

Refreshments: Have each lady bring a loaf of her special bread or half a dozen of her favorite Christmas cookies.

Song: "Joy to the World!"

Prayer: Dear Heavenly Father, we ask You to quiet our hearts that we may forget for a time the frenzy of the world. Help us to lift our hearts in praise to You for the gift of Your Son. We dedicate this time to You and pray that we may glorify You in our songs and contemplation of the season. We thank You for each one of the homes represented here today and pray our hearts will be open to Your teaching and leading. In Jesus' name, amen.

Scripture: Luke 2:1-20

Song: "What Child Is This?"

Heaven Touched Earth

"But made himself nothing, taking the very nature of a servant, being made in human likeness" (Philippians 2:7).

God came to earth! He didn't come to conquer the world but the hearts of men. There were no big announcements to the political leaders of His coming; only angels telling shepherds on a hill.

There was no media coverage of this great event. No town criers shouting the news of His coming; only the soft lowing of animals greeted God's arrival. The first visitors were not the influential people of the day, only the shepherds from the hills. Quietly, in a stable, God came to earth. God came and was wrapped in swaddling clothes.

God reaches down to man. Christianity is a personal relationship with a loving God. God brought Heaven and earth together by stretching out His Son on a cruel Roman cross where He became a sacrifice for man's sin. After His crucifixion, He rose from the dead and went back to glory.

Because of His sacrifice we can rejoice in the true meaning of Christmas. Heaven touched earth and we can find God's peace and spiritual freedom.
(Used by permission of *Moments with God* printed December 1986.)

Song: "Thou Didst Leave Thy Throne"

Perfect Gift

"God so loved the world that he gave his one and only Son" (John 3:16).

The clothespin soldier grins at a ceramic mouse in a stocking and the handmade felt animals blossom on the tree. A white dove nests under the angel and a beaded snowflake twirls listlessly.

Strings of lights shine on the little village placed on the mantel. The manger scene has its place of prominence and candy canes hang from the stockings. Gaily wrapped presents are heaped under the tree.

We watch our loved ones open the presents we have given, willing them to hurry. At last the gift is open and we search their eyes for a response. Is it the right color, the proper size, should I have gotten something else? A perfunctory thank you and the gift is put aside. Why didn't they like it? Sadness clouds our vision. We shopped carefully, chose the right paper and a big bow to give the final touch, but our present was rejected.

The perfect gift was not placed under an evergreen tree or in a box filled with tissue or Styrofoam nuggets. The perfect gift was not wrapped with special paper and a fancy bow. The perfect gift was not purchased at a well-known store or an out-of-the-way boutique. God prepared the one perfect gift suitable for any occasion, the gift of His Son. What have you done with God's Gift?
(Used by permission of *Moments with God* printed December 1986.)

Song: "Silent Night"

Meditation

Changed by God's Gift

Let's pause, quiet our hearts, and walk into a typical scene on one of our Western-style Christmas cards. Observe the silent beauty in God's forest. Notice the distant snow-tipped mountains are like a blue smudge against a gray sky, trees with their snow frosting sparkle, and fluffy snowflakes drifting lazily down. Brush the snow off a fallen tree and rest.

Our Christmas card portrays peace, but our actions mock this. What is the reason for the flurry of activity that invades us in December? We trim the outside of our home with Christmas lights and hang a wreath of evergreen boughs to brighten our entryway. Candlelight sheds it's warm glow on our mantels. Thinking of our home, we picture the tinsel-draped tree which is poor competition for God's natural beauty in our forest. The angels on our tree are silent and the manger scene only porcelain or plastic figures. Presents are stacked under the tree and candy canes twirl temptingly. Can we learn from these material things?

We believers want to focus our Christmas around the manger scene and we display it prominently in our homes. We romanticize the crude reality of the stable, forgetting primitive conditions. We need to remember the innkeeper was the victim of a bad press and not really cruel or unsympathetic. He was a tool, used by God, when he offered what room he had, a stable.

The world today makes little room for Christ even during the season of His birth. We offer cookies and holiday breads instead of making room for Him in our hearts. We get so engrossed celebrating Christ's birth we shut and bar the door to Christ.

Night has overcome dusk in our forest now. No tinsel on a tree can compare with the stars that glitter down on the tops of the forest giants which whisper and sigh in the gentle wind above us. Did the shepherds gathered by their sheep notice the star shining over Bethlehem? How terrified the men must have been when the angel of the Lord appeared. As they trembled with fear, it must have been hard to concentrate on what the angel said. The words, "Do not be afraid," did little to calm their fast-beating hearts. Christ the Lord is born, find Him ... in a manger. Then a great company of angels appeared with the angel praising God. As suddenly as it happened, the angels were gone. The night was still again. The shepherds must have looked at one another in wonder. Was it a dream? Did it really happen? The shepherds didn't sit and reflect on how wonderful it was to have seen the angels. They hurried off to find for themselves Christ the Lord. Their lives were changed.

The cold in our Christmas card penetrates us after sitting still and our minds wander. Time is fleeing, there is so much to do yet, presents to wrap or finish making.

Presents. That's a whole new thought. The outside wrapping on the packages are intriguing, but sometimes the contents disappoint us. Some gifts are only given because we know someone will give to us and not because we really want to give.

Our gifts are much different from those the Wise-men later brought to the young Child. Gold, a standard of money, was a gift given to royalty and only the wealthy could afford to give it. Frankincense, a fragrant gum, was taken from a tree in Arabia, mixed with the offerings of the priests and a gift of worship. Myrrh was used to anoint kings, given to those dying on a cross or mixed with aloes and sprinkled on burial cloth. A gift that meant suffering.

It's time to leave our Christmas card forest. Will we go through all the mechanics of getting our home ready for Christmas and neglect to prepare our hearts? Will we abuse our bodies by not eating properly and forget to feed our souls? Will our dream expectations of Christmas be so unrealistic we have a big letdown? Will we try to fill the emptiness of our life with worldly things? Instead let's prepare our hearts for Christmas by more prayer time, Bible study, and reflection on the true meaning of Christmas. Let's have the inside of our souls shine brighter than any Christmas decoration.

God, the Creator, wants us to open the doors of our hearts and accept the gift of His Son. Let's reflect on His gift to us. Of course, the gift isn't ours until we take it and if we have accepted God's gift, there is so much more He wants to give us.

Christmas can continue to make a difference in our lives even after all the decorations are put away for another year. We don't want to wrap Jesus up in tissue paper, along with the nativity scene, and not think much about Him until next Christmas or our next crisis. We can share the good news of His coming with others, not only at Christmas but throughout the year. We want our lives changed forever by God's gift to us.

Taking Action: Weren't you amazed with the list in your journal listing how many things for which you are thankful? This long list makes for a grateful heart. This month, let's spend extra time in prayer thanking God for His Gift. In your journal write down new insights and reasons why this Christmas is special. Have the ladies bring a gift for others in need in the local church body or food bank.

Read the book of 1 Peter in preparation for the program for next month.

Prayer: Dear Heavenly Father, help us remember the reason for celebrating Christmas and to spend more time in prayer. Let us not become so busy with the trivial things that we forget Your perfect Gift. Help us to use this season to share the Good News with others. We ask this in Jesus' name, amen.

Song: "O Come, All Ye Faithful"

Refreshments: Enjoy this time of fellowship during this special season.

God's Gift

>God's gift of love He gave the world,
>Wrapped in swaddling clothes.
>God's love gift in a manger lay
>Highlighted by a star.
>
>Wise-men gave their gold and myrrh
>And knelt before the baby.
>They could not match God's gift to us
>Wrapped in swaddling clothes.

Program 5

Changed by Bible Study

Name Tag

Program Outline

     Song: "Wonderful Words of Life"
    Prayer
   Scripture: 2 Timothy 3:16; Romans 12:2; 2 Corinthians 4:16; Philippians 4:8
Program Feature: Bible Study
 Taking Action: Continue journal, new Bible study techniques
    Prayer
    Song: "Standing on the Promises"
 Refreshments: Cake in shape of book
  Decorations: Winter theme, snowmen using different topics found in 1 Peter

Name Tags may be made using the sample provided here.

Decorations: Use a winter theme. Snowmen used later in the meeting may be placed around the room. *(See the example for ideas.)* The Scripture verses for today's program may be printed on these.

Refreshments: Depending on size of the group, 2 rectangular cakes could be stacked, then decorated white with gold sides and ends. A ribbon could come out of the ends of the Bible. Use gold frosting for lettering on the Bible.

Song: "Wonderful Words of Life"

Prayer: Dear Heavenly Father, we thank You for this time together. We pray our minds will be open so we can be changed by Bible study as we learn how to dig deeper into Your Word. We don't want this to be an intellectual exercise but a tool whereby we can learn more about You and how to apply Biblical truths to our daily lives. We ask these things in Jesus' name, amen.

Scripture: 2 Timothy 3:16; Romans 12:2; 2 Corinthians 4:16; Philippians 4:8

Program Feature

Leader: We want to determine how Bible study is different from devotional reading and meditation.

What is devotional reading?
   (Answer.) It is usually short, gives a lift for the day.

What is Bible study?

(Answer.) Careful reading and involvement of the Scriptures.

How can we be changed by Bible study? Jeremiah said when God's words came, "I ate them; they were my joy and my heart's delight" Jeremiah 15:16.
(Answer.) To see things from God's perspective, to know God's thoughts, to renew our minds. It isn't intellectual knowledge but meeting God in the pages of His letter to us. It is aligning ourselves with truth.

We don't want to slip and slide over God's words like we are on skis but use them to build snow forts to protect us from the world. We want to be teachable, humble, and cleansed from sin. We should not have preconceived ideas about what we are going to read and we should always acknowledge our dependence on God.
On a chalkboard or large sheet of paper write P E T E R, horizontally.
Look through the first chapter of 1 Peter and look for words starting with the letter P. *(They will find words like Praise, Peace, Perish, Prophets, Prediction, Prepare, Precious, Purified. There are no wrong answers!)*
Which word portrays the whole chapter to you? The word you select today might be different than the word you would choose a year from now.
Under the letter P write vertically the word Praise.
You could also use a word not found in the chapter that symbolizes the content to you. Perhaps Person referring to Christ. Look through the second chapter of 1 Peter and look for words starting with the letter E *(Evil, Endure, Entrust, Example)*. Again, which word portrays the chapter to YOU? Today, let's choose Example.
If time allows, go through the other chapters. Chapter 3 *(Talk, Tongue, Turn, or use Trials which typifies some of the subject matter)*

Chapter Four *(Earthly life, End, or Evil to Ecstasy)*

Chapter Five *(Revealed, Receive, Roaring, Resist* or *Responsibilities is a good word.)*

Your completed row of icicles could look like this.

```
P    E    T    E    R
R    X    R    V    E
A    A    I    I    S
I    M    A    L    P
S    P    L         O
E    L    S    T    N
     E         O    S
                    I
               E    B
               C    I
               S    L
               T    I
               A    T
               S    I
               Y    E
                    S
```

Choose words with special meanings for you. Then it is easier to remember the content of 1 Peter.

To build a snowman, take one of the words from your snow fort and build a snowman by searching through each of the five chapters to see if the topic is used. *(The snowmen could be used as decorations and reproduced on a take-home sheet.)* The topic is printed on the scarf, the numbers signify the chapters and the words tell how the topic is used.

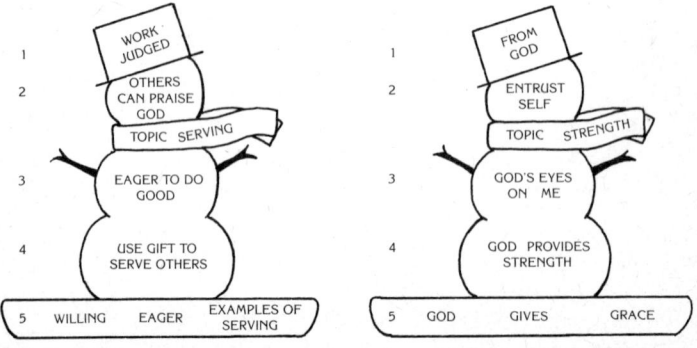

34

Because not all books work out like 1 Peter there are other ways. If the book has a lot of chapters or just has a few you could use one of the following ideas. *(You may use this as a take-home paper.)*

If there are more letters in the book title than number of chapters, you can abbreviate the name. *(Example Habakkuk.)*
H   arping
A   nswers
B   eseech

If there are more chapters than letters in the name, you may use words that apply to contents.

For example AMOS has 9 chapters, you could use shepherds or Daniel has 12 chapters so use fiery furnace.

If there are more chapters than letters in the name, you may group the chapters as shown here.
L evi or Law 1-7
E phod 8-10
V ittles 11-15
I ntercessor 16-17
T aboos 18-20
I nstructions 21-24
C onsecrate 25
U ltimation 26
S acred use 27

You may also organize by subject as shown here:

Joel	Galatians
B ugs	F ake gospel
U nfaithful	R evelation
G uilty	U nderstanding
	I saac
	T reasure
	S owing

Leader: Through faithful Bible study we will be changed when we apply the truths we learn.

Let's go back to the first chapter. How can we apply the P word, *Praise* to our lives? *(Answer)* Many times during the

35

day we can praise God for who He is and what He is doing in our lives.

In the second chapter, Christ is our Example. How are we measuring up? What kind of example are we setting? Are there areas we need to change?

Taking Action: Hasn't the extra time spent in prayer this past month made a change in your prayer life? Go back and reread the entries in your journal about why Christmas was special. Doing this will brighten the next few months. This coming month practice what you have learned about Bible study today and apply it to another book of the Bible.

Prayer: Dear Heavenly Father, we thank You for this time together. We have heard so much in such a short time but help us to use and apply some of what we learned so we may know more of You as You are revealed in Your Word. Give each of us an excitement to set aside time to study Your Word and to apply it to our lives. We thank You in Jesus' precious name, amen.

Song: "Standing on the Promises"

Refreshments: Enjoy the fellowship along with the cake, coffee, and tea.

MY BIBLE

My Bible's an open book,
The pages marked and worn.
Favorite words comfort me
And challenges there I find.

Heroes march across the page.
Villains are clearly displayed.
I see Jesus walking there
All the way to Calvary.

Renew my mind, dear Father
Through Your inspired thoughts.
May I thirst for Your wisdom
And revel in Your Word.

Program 6

Changed by Love

Name Tag

Program Outline

              Song: "More Like the Master"
            Prayer
       Scripture: 1 John 3:7-24
Program Feature: Soap Opera, "As the Wall Stands"
     Discussion
  Taking Action: Take the first step to show love to that unlovable one.
           Prayer
            Song: "Make Me a Blessing"
  Refreshments: Heart-shaped cookies or cake
    Decorations: Hearts

Name Tags may be made using the sample provided here. Be sure to introduce guests and help them to feel welcome.

Refreshments: Heart-shaped cookies or cake

Decorations: Print the sayings on page 41 on heart shaped posters placed around the room. These will be used later in the program.

Song: "More Like the Master"

Prayer: Dear Heavenly Father, today we are going to focus our attention on love. May our minds be open so we may truly understand what love is. We each have someone in our life we find difficult to love at times. We can't do it on our own. Help us to be channels for Your love to flow through us. We want to be able to feel the depth of Your love for us. In Jesus' name, amen.

Scripture: 1 John 3:7-24

Soap Opera Cast: Announcer, Dizzy, Mizzy

Setting: If possible, draw a picture of a rock wall on butcher paper. Label some of the rocks pride, self-pity, and so forth. Make three of the "rocks" removable. Dizzy and Mizzy are seated at a table drinking coffee. Background music can be played during the time the announcer is speaking to help set the mood for the scene.

Announcer: We are standing in front of the beautiful wall that Dizzy and Tizzy built. Hand hewn stones were carefully fitted into place. Dizzy and Tizzy spent so much time working on this wall they didn't look around and realize they were on opposite sides of the wall until it was finished. We have watched Dizzy bang on the wall, but Tizzy doesn't pay much attention. Today we find Dizzy by the wall talking and drinking coffee with her friend Mizzy.

Dizzy: I'm frustrated with this wall. I used to have a close relationship with Tizzy and I miss that. We were out in our field one day and dropped a few stones. We then started piling them up. Somehow they got too high. I can't push the wall over or even see Tizzy on the other side. Yesterday I tried going around the end and the thorns of rejection dug into me and I had to turn back.

Mizzy: What about the other end of the wall?
Dizzy: There is a steep cliff and I'd need climbing gear to climb it and I don't have any.
Mizzy: What about tearing the wall down?
Dizzy: I tried banging on the wall with a crowbar of hostility but all it did was bruise my hands. *(Looks at hands.)* I've tried everything. *(Slumps in chair or puts head in hands.)*
Mizzy: Have you really tried everything?
Dizzy: I don't know what else to do.
Mizzy: Why don't you plant these seeds by your wall?
Dizzy: I'm having a horrible time in my life and you want me to plant some dumb seeds. What a friend you are! What kind of seeds? *(Looks over the package.)* Love seeds! You've got to be kidding.
Mizzy: You said you've tried everything else. Why don't you try this? It isn't going to happen overnight, but it will work.
Announcer *(dramatically):* Dizzy took the seeds and planted them by her wall. She watered them with the tears of self-pity. Is Mizzy right? Will the love seeds work? Tune in tomorrow.

Leader: Do you have a wall between you and someone else? What kind of wall? What kinds of stones have you added to the wall?

Discussion: Direct the discussion to include some of the words printed on the rocks that can build a wall between people.

Last of Soap Opera

Announcer: It has been some time since Dizzy planted the love vine seeds. Again we find Dizzy out by her wall with Mizzy.
Mizzy: Your love vine has really grown. Did you notice the small piles of mortar at the base of your wall? Those little tendrils are breaking up the mortar of vanity.
Dizzy: You're right. Those tendrils from the vine are doing what my crowbar of hostility couldn't do. *(She stands up by the wall.)* This rock of self-righteousness moves.
Mizzy: Can you take it out? I'll help if you want.
Dizzy: No, I got it. I can see Tizzy over there.

Mizzy: What's he doing? Does he look pleased?

Dizzy: He's just standing there. He doesn't look displeased. Why doesn't he come over and help me. This stone of self-pity is loose too, and the rock of pride. *(Hands rock to Mizzy.)*

Mizzy: That love vine is really working.

Dizzy: Wait a minute. If I take these down and Tizzy doesn't help, Tizzy will think I'm the one to blame for everything. *(Starts to put them back.)*

Mizzy: Don't put them back. Somebody has to start taking down the wall.

Dizzy: It doesn't have to be me. Hand me the rock of pride. I'm really going to shove it in.

Mizzy *(protests):* But the love vine was really doing something.

Dizzy: I'm not ready yet. I'm always the one who makes the first move and tries to make peace. Why can't Tizzy make the first move just this once.

Mizzy: That's how it is many times. By the way, I brought you another present.

Dizzy: What is it this time?

(Mizzy hands package to Dizzy.)

Dizzy: More seeds!

Mizzy: Yes. These are special seeds of faith. I'm sure they will do the same thing the love vine is doing. If they don't break down the wall, at least the two vines will grow big and strong. Then you will be able to climb up over the wall on them.

Dizzy: Why would I want to do that?

Mizzy: I heard you say you wanted that close relationship with Tizzy again.

Dizzy: Yeah, but Tizzy doesn't.

Mizzy: We can't change others, we can only change ourselves.

Dizzy *(resistance gone):* Okay, help me plant the seeds of faith.

Announcer: We leave Dizzy and Mizzy by the wall. *(Dramatically.)* Can love and faith break down the wall? Will Dizzy remove the stones of pride, self-pity and self-righteousness and leave them out? Will Tizzy decide to help take down the wall? What do you think?

Discussion

Leader: How do you show love when the other person doesn't seem to respond? *(After receiving a few answers, continue on.)*

Let's learn more about love. We'll go around the room and read what it says on the posters about love. Explain what it means to you. If others have something else to add, please do so. *(If you aren't using the poster idea, have the words printed on slips of paper to be passed out. A starter thought for the leader follows each statement if it is needed.)*

- LOVE IS A COMMITMENT. In marriage, it involves every part of me. A steadfast commitment.
- LOVE IS GOD'S COMMAND. Matthew 5:44; 1 John 4:20; 1 John 3:23. Love is a learned response even if feelings and emotions don't change immediately.
- LOVE IS A CHOICE. Love is a decision, not an emotion but an act of the will. We can love someone even if we don't approve of all their behavior. We accept imperfections. Love is a decision otherwise God would not command it.
- LOVE IS BEING QUIET WHEN WORDS WOULD HURT. It's not constantly talking about a problem; it doesn't bring up the past. It's responding with a soft answer.
- LOVE IS SHADE ON A HOT DAY. Are you a comfort to others, a listener?
- LOVE IS A LONG-TERM INVESTMENT. It's a slow bearing fruit; you don't always see results at first, but God is at work.
- LOVE DOESN'T QUIT. It doesn't quit when the going is hard. Galatians 6:7-9.
- LOVE IS SHARING THE LAST COOKIE. It is self-denying, going somewhere when you would prefer another place.
- LOVE IS A MAGNET. Draws others to you.
- LOVE IS A GIFT. Wants to meet the needs of others, looks for their best interest, gives best of self.
- LOVE ADDS THAT EXTRA TOUCH. Duty fixes dinner, love makes a favorite dessert.
- LOVE IS UNCONDITIONAL. You don't love someone *because* he does something or *if* he does something. It is not dependent on how love is received.

LOVE IS LOYAL. It doesn't tear down or expose another's weakness.
LOVE IS NEVER DEPLETED. Always more divine love spills out and nourishes us and our love to others. Romans 5:5.
LOVE LOSES A PENCIL. It doesn't keep track of wrongs.
LOVE GIVES BENEFIT OF DOUBT. Gives others best motive.
LOVE IS A CHANNEL. It can flow through us.

Taking Action: Didn't you enjoy trying a new method of Bible study this past month? Does your journal show the results?

Our topic this month is "What does love mean to you?" In your journal write down three things about love. Take the first step to show love to someone in your life who is difficult to love. Be sure to write down the marvelous change this brings in that person's life.

Prayer: Dear Heavenly Father, help me become the woman You want me to be. Help me to love unconditionally since this is the way You love me. Help me to look for the good qualities in others, to love in a new and deeper way, to take an interest in what another person likes and try to imagine how that person feels. We ask this in Jesus' name, amen.

Song: "Make Me a Blessing"

Refreshments: Enjoy the fellowship this time of refreshments provides.

Love Has No Strings Attached

Love is more than hearts and flowers,
Or moonlight on a summer night.
Love is more than mere emotions.
It blooms with tender care.

Love has no strings attached to it,
Or great expectations.
Love is a decision we make.
It adds a special touch.

Program 7

Changed by Prayer

Name Tag

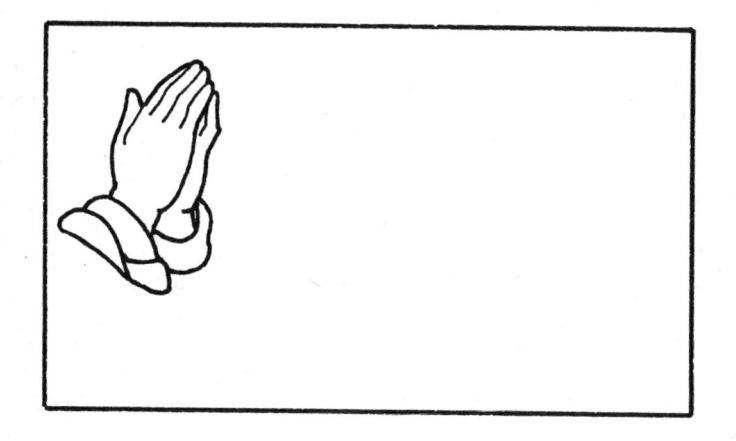

Program Outline

Song: "Sweet Hour of Prayer"
Scripture: 1 Chronicles 29:10-13
Prayer
Program Feature: Different parts of prayer.
Taking Action: Writing letters to the Lord.
Prayer
Song: "Teach Me to Pray"
Refreshments: Gingerbread and whipped cream
Decorations: Boxes marked with ADORATION, CONFESSION, etc. around the room and a prayer chart.

Name Tags may be made using the sample provided here. Introduce guests and make sure they are included in activities.

Decorations: Make a prayer chart. Use boxes or posters to look like boxes marked with ADORATION, CONFESSION, RESTING, FORGIVENESS, BIBLE READING, LISTEN, INTERCESSION, PRAYER PETITIONS, PRAISE.

Refreshments: Old-fashioned gingerbread with whipped cream and beverage

Song: "Sweet Hour of Prayer"

Scripture: 1 Chronicles 29:10-13

Prayer: Dear Heavenly Father, we come to You asking to learn more about prayer and how we can better communicate with You. Help us to realize if we have open and willing hearts, You will hear and answer our prayers. Help us to open our inner hearts and minds to You. In Jesus' name, amen.

Leader: Quiz Questions. *(Pass out paper.)* You may write down your answers, however, they are only for you. You don't need to share the answers.
1. Why do you pray?
2. How much time do you spend in prayer daily?
3. What are your barriers to more prayer time? Are you too busy, don't want to get up early, or would rather watch TV, or something else?
4. Which of these barriers are really excuses?

(Leader has an overnight bag with boxes marked with the different parts of prayer in it. To involve others you could have a different lady tell about each box. Let them know ahead of time they will be doing this. As each lady comes forward to tell about her part of prayer, have her remove the box marked with her word from the bag. She could also write her word on the chalkboard so all the words will be listed when you are finished.) We are going to look at the different parts of prayer. If you don't pray in this sequence, it doesn't mean you are wrong. These are suggestions to help you have a more meaningful prayer.

FIRST BOX: ADORATION

Close your eyes and imagine a throne room. Tall mirrors catch and bounce back the gold and other rich colors in the room. Tall windows are richly draped in velvet. Chairs are lined up on the sides of the room. The ornate throne sits on a platform. Jesus is King of kings and Lord of lords. Even though our Creator and God of the universe sits on the throne, He longs for us to come into His presence.

"Yours, O Lord, is the greatness and the power and the glory and the majesty and the splendor, for everything in heaven and earth is yours. Yours, O Lord, is the kingdom; you are exalted as head over all. Wealth and honor come from you; you are the ruler of all things. In your hands are strength and power to exalt and give strength to all. Now, our God, we give you thanks, and praise your glorious name" (1 Chronicles 29:11-13).

Sing Chorus: "Majesty, Come Worship His Majesty"

SECOND BOX: RESTING

Rest in His presence. Resting means not talking, meditating or listening, but letting God give you a hug and feeling God's presence. Prayer is cuddling up in the arms of God.

"Be still, and know that I am God" (Psalm 46:10). Take time to sit on God's lap. *(Allow silent time to practice "resting.")*

THIRD BOX: CONFESSION

(Third lady hands out pieces of paper.)

Because God is a holy God, we need to come to Him in honesty and humility and with a clean heart. If God would shine a searchlight into our hearts, would He find a critical, worrying, or complaining spirit? Would He find envy, anger, pride, impatience, self-pity, a headstrong attitude, or unbelief? We would need to confess these sins. Confessing is agreeing with God that we have done something wrong. We do not sin against others but against God.

"Against you, you only, have I sinned and done what is evil in your sight, so that you are proved right when you speak and justified when you judge" (Psalm 51:4).

On the paper I gave you, list the sins you are aware of in your life right now. *(Allow time for the ladies to list the sins on the paper that was handed out.)*

FOURTH BOX: FORGIVENESS

It is impossible to go through life without being hurt physically or mentally. People ask for our forgiveness and many times we say outwardly we forgive them, but we hold onto that hurt and resentment. Sometimes we even take pleasure in being angry with someone. Let's take time and ask God to forgive us for the sins we have listed on our paper. *(A silent time so they may ask forgiveness.)*

"He is faithful and just and will forgive us our sins" (1 John 1:9).

Now write PAID IN FULL over your list of sins. We have just asked God to forgive us. Since He has forgiven us, how can we withhold our forgiveness from someone else? We may not be aware of our hidden anger. Let us close our eyes and think about someone we need to forgive and hidden anger we need to be rid of. May we ask God to help us do this. *(Allow a silent time for contemplation.)*

FIFTH BOX: BIBLE READING

The Bible provides travel information and is our road map. God speaks to us through His Word so we can avoid costly detours. When we travel by car we stop at service stations to check the oil and gas levels in our vehicles so they will run smoothly. The Bible is fuel for our souls and gives us the right perspective. Ask the Lord to help you use your Bible each day as a guide as you travel through life. Consider how to apply these spiritual truths you learn to your everyday life.

SIXTH BOX: LISTEN

Allow God to communicate with us. When we visit friends, we give them an opportunity to speak. So it is with prayer. Stop talking. Ask for directions. Wait. Have paper and pencil handy. If we don't hear a message during our prayer time,

God may communicate with us during the day through remembered Bible verse or thoughts. He may put someone into our minds we should call. As He sees our needs, He will encourage, strengthen, rebuke, or inspire us. Take time to LISTEN.

SEVENTH BOX: INTERCESSION

When we pray for others, we are releasing God's power. Believe He is working in our friends and loved ones even if we can't see a change. We can't see God's hand giving a planted seed life anymore than we can see God working in lives.

We don't want to try and bend God's will to ours but help create a new situation in which God uses us as His instruments. We can focus on the positive aspects of our loved ones, not the negative quirks of their personalities and habits. Thank the Lord the answer is on the way. However, we may not be ready for the answer. If a child asks for a pocket knife and he is too young, the wise parent will say no until he is old enough to use it correctly. Sometimes we may not be ready for God's answer and must wait, or perhaps God has something better planned. Let's take a few moments to pray for someone.

EIGHTH BOX: PRAYER PETITIONS

Petitions are for ourselves, for guidance for the next day, for willing and obedient hearts or for our physical needs.

Let's close our eyes and pray as you follow my words. Imagine we are in a boat with Jesus. He rows a little way from shore. The only sound is the quiet slapping of the waves gently hitting the boat. Jesus has all the time you need to listen to your concerns. Talk with Him. *(Take a few minutes and then continue.)*

Do perplexing questions haunt you? Now is the time to ask. Confide in Him all your fears for the future. Pour out the hurts and disappointments that weigh you down. *(Again take a few minutes and then continue.)*

Still in the boat, dangle your fingers in the water. Look at the beauty and wonder of the world around you and thank Him for all the riches He has given you, His unfailing love. Thank Him for always being there to hear your prayer. *(Again pause and end with)* Amen.

NINTH BOX: PRAISE
 We began with praise and we end with praise. Believe God is in control. It is possible to live in a spirit of thanksgiving and praise even in the midst of problems. Problems can turn into blessings. Wait with eager assurance, knowing God will work in His own time and way. Thank God for the answer that is on the way. Let's thank and praise the Lord and I will close this time. *(Take a few minutes and then close with this prayer.)*
 Thank You, Lord, for this special time we have had today to spend in Your presence. May each of us leave excited about spending more time in prayer each day. Help us to lift up our hands to touch Your face, Lord. We ask in Jesus' name, amen.

Taking Action: We've been writing in our journals for six months now. Take time to go back and read your entries. Notice the changes that have taken place. Note the progress with loving the unlovable one in your life. Pray for that person during this next month. Write a letter to God each day, include definite prayer requests and the dates. Then you can record the answers when they happen.

Prayer: Again Lord, we come before Your throne thanking You for what we have been learning through these programs. Please change us by prayer. Thank You for the refreshments and the hands that prepared them. We pray in Jesus' name, amen.

Song: "Teach Me to Pray"

Refreshments: Serve the refreshments and enjoy this time of fellowship.

Prayer

P raise Him daily for His goodness.
R est in His presence today.
A cknowledge sins, He'll forgive.
Y earn for His will for you.
E xalt His precious name each day.
R ead His words and make them yours.

This may be prepared as a reminder of the parts of prayer and as a guide to a better prayer life.

The person who desires God more than His gifts is blessed.

CONDITIONS FOR PRAYER LIFE: A quiet place, a quiet heart, proper relationship with God and man.

ADORE: Delight yourself in the Lord. 1 Chronicles 29:11-13
REST: Let God give you a hug.
CONFESSION: I sin against God. Psalm 51:4
FORGIVENESS: God forgives me, I need to forgive others.
BIBLE READING: Let God speak to you through His Word.
LISTEN: Be still, let God speak to you through silence.
INTERCESSION: Pray for family, friends, government officials, and so forth.
PETITIONS: My needs. A willing obedient heart, guidance for today, physical needs.
PRAISE AND THANKSGIVING: Thank Him for your many blessings: His care, salvation, Scripture, nature, and so forth.

Using a small notebook, each day besides praying for family members and their relationships to God, list the people who influence your family and pray for them.

MONDAY: Pray for your family unit, for children to be teachable at home and school. Pray for friends, neighbors, co-workers, boss, and fellow employees.
TUESDAY: Pray for school teachers, club leaders, coaches, music teacher, others in regular contact with children.
WEDNESDAY: Pray for those in leadership positions in local government: mayor, county officials, city council, state legislators.
THURSDAY: Pray for national leaders, President, Vice-president, senators, representatives, Supreme Court.
FRIDAY: Pray for the missionaries, for their witness, to be able to speak boldly and clearly, that the Lord would open doors for them.
SATURDAY: Pray for church leaders, ministers, teachers, choir director.
SUNDAY: Spend time in worship and praise.

Program 8 — Changed Appearance

Name Tag

Program Outline

                Song: "I Would Be Like Jesus"
          Scripture: Colossians 3:12-14
              Prayer
Program Feature: Style show
   Taking Action: Focus on the 7 words in Colossians 3:12-14. How do you see these words applied in your life?
              Prayer
                Song: "Christ Liveth in Me"
     Decorations: Butterflies, spring flowers
   Refreshments: Fruit platter, butterfly-shaped cake.

Name Tags may be made using the sample idea provided here. Be sure to introduce and include all guests in the activities.

Decorations: Spring flowers and paper butterflies placed around the room.

Refreshments: Fruit platter, butterfly-shaped cake. Take a round cake and cut it in half. Put the rounded sides together to form a butterfly. Decorate the wings with the color of any spring flowers you are using.

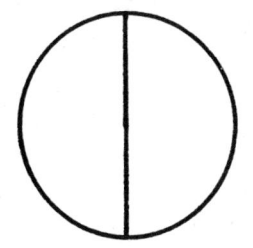

Song: "I Would Be Like Jesus"

Scripture: Colossians 3:12-14

Prayer: Dear Heavenly Father, today we are talking about changing our appearance. As a butterfly is in the chrysalis or formative stage, so we are as believers in our chrysalis stage of Christian development. Help us to realize what accessories are missing in our lives for that important inner beauty. We ask in Jesus' name, amen.

Program Feature

Leader: Today we are going to be discussing beauty by combining it with a study of accessories. Most of us have at least one thing we would like to change about our physical bodies. We think we are too short, too tall, too skinny, or too fat. Our nose is too large or too small. We don't like the color of our hair or it's too fine or too coarse in texture. Our fingers are stubby, our feet too long, our eyes nearsighted or farsighted or our skin is full of blemishes. What can we do?

Instead of bemoaning our faults, we are going to enhance ourselves. We can't do anything about our height, but we can wear clothes that don't call undue attention to our figure faults. We can determine the length and color of our hair. We can style it to distract attention away from our less than perfect feature. We can't change our vision, but we can shape our eyebrows, wear eye make-up or even change the color of our eyes with contact lenses. We can use cosmetics to cover up blemishes in our skin and add color to highlight our natural beauty to make us more attractive.

Misfit *(Enters wearing a football helmet with the word ANGER written on it; an ugly, bright, bold, scarf with the word RAGE written on it; a big pointy pin made out of paper with the word MALICE written on it. She carries a big purse with a card taped to the outside that says SLANDER. She is wearing a black paper chain belt with the words BAD LANGUAGE written on it and the word LIES written on the shoes.):* Is this the place where they are going to talk about beauty and accessories?

Leader: We are going to discuss what beauty means and how to combine it with accessories for spring. May I say, you have some very unusual accessories.

Misfit: Why, thank you. I picked them out myself.

Leader: Would you like to sit down and talk about some accessories from our fashion book?

Misfit: Yes, that would be nice. What book do you use? *(Starts to sit down.)*

Leader: We are using the Bible.

Misfit: The Bible! *(Jumps up.)* You've got to be kidding. The Bible doesn't talk about accessories or teach fashion.

Leader: If you would like to join us, I think you will find there are some fashion tips for us.

Misfit: I don't believe you will be able to change my mind, but I'll sit and listen. *(Takes a seat in front near leader and slouches down. There is a box of other accessories beside her. She will use them later.)*

Leader: Webster's dictionary says, beauty is "whatever pleases or satisfies the senses or mind;" "very pleasing to the eye, ear, mind;" or "that which gives the highest degree of pleasure."

1. What makes a person beautiful? *(Write down answers on chalkboard.)*
2. What qualities make someone beautiful? *(Write down answers.)*

We will begin our style show now. Our first model is featuring a hat.

Misfit *(jumps up):* How do you like my hat?

Leader: Well, it's certainly different. Unique. Why are you wearing a football helmet?

Misfit: Why it's the latest in combative millinery accessories. Don't you read the fashion magazines? The brand name is ANGER.

Leader: Yes, I see that. *(The leader acts unsure about what to do with Misfit.)* All of our models are featuring the accessories mentioned in Colossians 3:12-14. *(Reads it aloud.)* Here is our first model, Miss COMPASSION.

(COMPASSION enters with pretty spring hat. The word Compassion is written on a card she carries. The Leader describes the hat in "fashion language." After everyone has seen the hat, COMPASSION sits down in a row of chairs facing the audience.)

Leader: Next we will see the latest in scarves. *(KINDNESS enters wearing a pretty scarf and carries a card with Kindness written on it. Leader describes the scarf in "fashion language.")*

Leader: Thank you.
   (KINDNESS sits down beside COMPASSION.)

Leader: HUMILITY will be showing us some jewelry, a pin. *(Describes pin as HUMILITY enters and shows pin. She carries a card with Humility written on it, sits with other models.)*

Leader: Our next model features a belt of GENTLENESS. *(Describes the belt, a soft cloth belt would be best, as GENTLENESS enters, carries card with Gentleness written on it. Sits with other models.)*

Leader: Thank you, GENTLENESS. The next accessory we are going to look at is a purse. PATIENCE is our next model.
   (PATIENCE enters, carries card with Patience written on it. Shows purse and sits by other models.)

Leader: Thank you, PATIENCE.

Leader *(looks at list):* We have another model, FORGIVENESS would you come out please. She has a pair of nice shoes. *(Describes shoes in "fashion language" as FORGIVENESS enters, shows off shoes, and sits with other models.)*

Leader: Thank you, FORGIVENESS. Now we will go on with our program.

Love *(from offstage tries to get Leader's attention):* Don't forget me.

Leader: Of course, I can't forget our last model, LOVE. The one accessory we shouldn't be without. *(LOVE enters as leader describes shawl or cape made out of a see through material like net. LOVE models the cape and sits with other models.)*

Leader: Now we have everyone. *(Turns to Misfit.)* What do you think of these accessories?

Misfit: They are certainly different than mine. *(Looks down at hers.)* I think I would like to hear more about them.

Leader: That sounds like a good idea. We'll go back and let each of our models tell us a little more about her accessory. COMPASSION would you begin please.

Compassion: The story is told of the good Samaritan who passed a man who had been beaten and robbed.

"When he saw him, he took pity on him. He went to him and bandaged his wounds, pouring on oil and wine. Then he put the man on his own donkey, took him to an inn and took care of him" (Luke 10:33, 34).

We may be in a similar situation to the good Samaritan where we can help someone in need. We are told to "Carry each other's burdens, and in this way you will fulfill the law of Christ" (Galatians 6:2).

Leader: Thank you. *(Ask the audience this question for discussion.)* How can we show compassion today? *(You can write down answers on the chalkboard. The following thoughts can be added to the answers given by the ladies.)*

To sum it up, compassion is not just a forgiving attitude but it is to feel deeply for another. It is sympathy and tenderness toward someone who is suffering. It can be compared to walking in another person's shoes, trying to feel what she feels.

Misfit *(takes off football helmet and takes out a pretty hat from her box. It has a streamer with COMPASSION written on it)*: This really is much nicer.
Leader: I see you've changed hats. That is much better. Isn't your scarf uncomfortable? It looks like it is strangling you.
Misfit: Rage does that to one.
Leader: Maybe you would be interested in hearing what KINDNESS has to say. She wears a different type of scarf. *(MISFIT feels her scarf, unties it, and sits down.)*
Leader: KINDNESS, what can you tell us?
Kindness: The good Samaritan showed kindness as did Joseph in Genesis 50:21. He had been sold by his brothers into slavery but later he spoke kindly to them.
Leader: Thank you. What are some ways we can show kindness today?
(Write down answers on chalkboard. The following thoughts can be added to what the ladies have shared.) Kindness and compassion work together in words and deeds. We can speak kindly and let others know they are valuable. We can protect another person's dignity. Kindness is a desire for another's well-being.

"Be devoted to one another in brotherly love. Honor one another above yourselves" (Romans 12:10).

Leader *(speaks to Misfit)*: What did you think of KINDNESS instead of RAGE?
Misfit: I've gotten rid of rage. Kindness is much more becoming. *(Has changed her scarf to one in soft colors.)* What was modeled next? Wasn't it about pins or jewelry? I wonder if I will like it better than my pin of malice?
Leader: Let's see what HUMILITY has to say.
Humility: Christ was the greatest example of humility. He gave up all the glories of Heaven to take the form of man so we might be saved.
Leader: Can you think of a lady in the Bible who demonstrated humility?
Humility: There was the Canaanite woman mentioned in Matthew 15:22. She came to ask Jesus to heal her daughter. He didn't pay any attention to her at first and the

disciples wanted Him to send her away. Jesus said He was sent to the people of Israel. She humbly asked for His help. Because of humility and faith, Jesus healed her daughter.

Leader: Thank you, HUMILITY. How can we show humility? *(Write down answers on chalkboard. Can add the following thoughts.)* We can't take a breath without God. That is a humbling thought. We don't have to prove ourselves to God. We don't have to be arrogant or self-assertive or call attention to ourselves. We can put the needs of others before our own. We can have a delicate consideration of the rights and feelings of others. If a believer is humble before the greatness of God, it will influence her attitude to others.

Misfit *(removes pin and exchanges it for a big paper flower with HUMILITY written on it):* I try to coordinate all my accessories but my belt of BAD LANGUAGE doesn't look right with my pin. At least the top half of my outfit is starting to look better. *(Sits down again and doesn't slouch as much.)*

Leader: Maybe GENTLENESS can help you change your belt.

Gentleness: God is gentle with us.

> "He tends his flock like a shepherd: He gathers the lambs in his arms and carries them close to his heart; he gently leads those that have young" (Isaiah 40:11).

> Gentleness is a quiet submission. It is not insisting on always having our own way. We are under God's control, we don't have to control others. Gentleness is like courtesy. It's a softness.

Misfit *(Changes her belt to a soft belt. Walks over with her purse to PATIENCE):* How do you like my purse?

Patience: It is big. It would hold a lot. Would you like to see mine again?

Misfit: Tell me about PATIENCE. *(Sits down.)*

Patience: "Perseverance must finish its work so that you may be mature and complete, not lacking anything" (James 1:4).

Leader: If God always answered prayer immediately instead of waiting, we would not be able to learn patience. Is there anyone here that would like to share examples of this? *(Give the ladies a chance to share and then sum it up.)* Patience doesn't wear a long face. It is a willingness to suffer with faults and unpleasantness even though it is irritating. Aren't we glad God has patience with us?

Misfit *(has changed her purse for a smaller one that says PATIENCE):* I'm just about completely outfitted now.

Leader: How does it feel?

Misfit: I feel different. Sort of nice but my shoes pinch.

Leader: Well, the brand name isn't the best, LIES.

Misfit: What would you suggest?

Leader: How about forgiveness? FORGIVENESS can you help her?

Forgiveness: "For if you forgive men when they sin against you, your heavenly Father will also forgive you" (Matthew 6:14).

Misfit: If I had forgiveness, my feet wouldn't be loaded down with the heaviness of lies.

Leader: What do you think that Scripture tells us about forgiveness?

Misfit: I had better forgive anyone who has wronged me or God won't forgive me.

Leader: Right. All we have to do is confess our sins and ask for forgiveness. " He is faithful and just and will forgive us our sins and purify us from all unrighteousness" (1 John 1:9). When we have unconfessed sin in our life, we lose our right relationship with God.

Misfit *(changes shoes):* That's better. You're right, the Bible does help us in the way we dress. I like my new look. There is one more thing I need. I like that cape. What is it called?

Leader: We need love. LOVE would you tell us about yourself?

Love: Love binds everything together. Without love all of the other things are moral attitudes. Love is the bond of perfection. We want to love as God loves us.

Leader *(asks audience):* In our February program we talked a lot about love. What happens if we try to be kind, compassionate, or patient without love? *(Write down answers on chalkboard.)* Does a loving person have a special beauty? What characteristics do you see in a loving person?

(Misfit puts on cape.)

Leader: How about a special thanks for all of our models and especially for Misfit. She can be an example for all of us. We want Christ's beauty to shine through us.

Taking Action: How's the journal keeping? Have you been writing letters to the Lord this last month?

Today we have seen the results of our fashion accessories. We need to do more than say, "Today I will be more compassionate." The more we read our Bible, pray, and allow God to work in our lives, the more understanding and loving we will become. This week let's spend one day thinking about Compassion. Think of an incident recently where you showed compassion or someone showed you compassion. The next day focus on Kindness, then Humility, then Gentleness, Patience, Forgiveness, and Love until you have gone through the list mentioned in Colossians 3:12-14. Then go through the list again. Write down the incidents and the results.

Prayer: Thank You, Lord, for this day You have given us. Help us to be like John the Baptist who recognized Jesus as the Lamb of God. He knew he must decrease and Christ increase. We want Christ to shine through us so others will be drawn to Him by our compassion and gentle spirit. We want Your love to be revealed through us. In Jesus' name, amen.

Song: "Christ Liveth in Me"

Refreshments: Serve the fruit platter or butterfly cake and beverages.

Proper Attire

Compassion understands.
Kindness wears a smile.
Humility stoops to help.
Gentleness is like butterfly wings.
Patience is losing a calendar.
Forgiveness always forgets.
Love makes all the difference.

Program 9

Changed by Serving

Name Tag

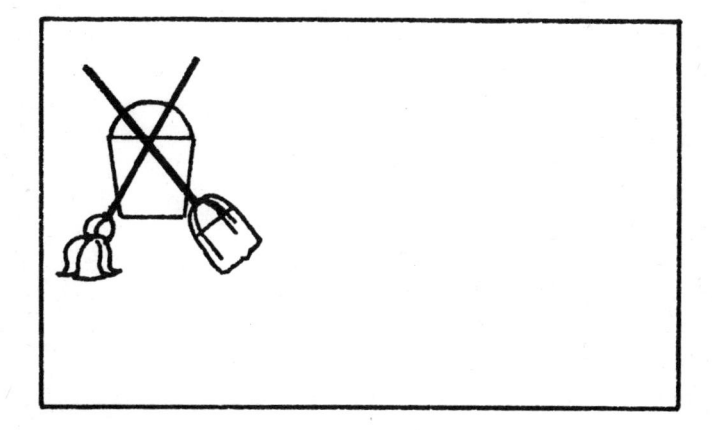

Program Outline

                Song: "Make Me a Channel of Blessing"
              Prayer
           Scripture: Luke 17:7-10
     Program Feature: Skit and Talk Time
       Taking Action: Evaluate your areas of service and see
                      where you can make changes.
              Prayer
                Song: "Oh Jesus, I Have Promised"
             Special: Recognize mothers and reading
              Prayer
         Decorations: Small buckets with a feather duster
        Refreshments: Sandwiches, vegetable tray

Name Tags may be made using the sample provided here. Be sure to introduce guests and include them in the activities.

Decorations: Small cleaning buckets with a feather duster, handle down, and flowers tucked in. These may be given as prizes during the mother recognition part of the program.

Refreshments: Sandwiches, fresh vegetable tray, and beverages

Song: "Make Me a Channel of Blessing"

Prayer: Dear Heavenly Father, we sang about being channels of blessings, but it is hard to know how to be those channels. We pray for a servant's heart and a real willingness to serve others in Your name. We pray in the name of Your precious Son, Jesus. Amen.

Scripture: Luke 17:7-10

Program Feature

Lady *(Comes out with a dirty apron on, scarf on her head, carrying bucket, mop, feather duster, and newspaper which could have her script on it. She can shuffle papers around to change pages as needed. She chews gum.):* Servants sure don't get coffee breaks around here. I'm up at the crack of dawn washing, scrubbing, cleaning, cooking, running all the time. No one ever notices I've done anything or thanks me.
Leader: Jesus called us to be servants.
Lady: Now just where do you find that?
Leader: Why Jesus said, He came to serve and not to be served.
Lady: Really, Jesus said that? So I'm serving. I'm really serving. I work all the time and no thanks, howdy do, or nothing. You try it for awhile.
Leader: I know it isn't easy, but listen to this. *(Reads Luke 17:7-10.)*

Lady: That gives one something to think about doesn't it? Only doing what's expected. But that fellow was doing something more important. He was out in the fields under the sun watching the miracle of plants growing from seeds or out caring for the flocks. All I do is clean up other people's messes.

Leader: Have you heard of Dorcas?

Lady: Doesn't she have a TV show on in the morning or is she on one of the soap operas?

Leader: No. She was mentioned in the Bible, in the book of Acts, chapter 9, verse 36.

Lady: Is this going to take a long time?

Leader: Not a lot of time, why?

Lady: Thought I would get comfortable if it's going to be a lecture-type thing. *(Turns bucket over and sits on it.)* Okay, I'm ready.

Leader: Dorcas was the only woman in the Bible called a disciple. Because she followed Jesus it made everything different in her life. She demonstrated her faith by serving others. She didn't feel that she could do very much. In those days women didn't have all the opportunities for service we have today. She did what she knew how to do, she sewed for the Lord. During bad weather many fishermen lost their lives so there were a lot of widows and orphans in Joppa. Dorcas sewed things that the widows and orphans needed. I bet she worked day and night even though she was tired. She was fulfilled knowing she was meeting the needs of others. She probably listened to them when they needed to talk.

Lady: That was fine for her. She did something pretty important. She saw babies and women wear the clothes she made. All I do is the same thing day after day; dishes, mopping floors, cleaning bathrooms. Wish I could do something important.

Leader: What I'm trying to say is this. It isn't important what we do; whether it is sewing, cooking, waiting on people in a store or cleaning. Our attitude in doing these jobs is the important thing.

Lady: My attitude is fine. If I get a hold of those kids that make such a mess and never put anything away, I'd show them my attitude. *(Moves like to spank or makes a fist.)*

Leader: Let's try something else. What about a mother's attitude?

Lady: Yeah, long hours, kids that get sick, driving them here and there for ball games, swimming lessons, piano lessons. Must be love, couldn't pay anyone else enough to do all that.

Leader: So it's attitude, right? I know what would change your approach to your job and make you eager to serve.

Lady: I doubt that, but go ahead and tell me. You will anyway.

Leader *(reads Colossians 3:23, 24):* "Whatever you do, work at it with all your heart, as working for the Lord, not for men, since you know that you will receive an inheritance from the Lord as a reward. It is the Lord Christ you are serving."

Lady: Work at it with all my heart. *(Pause.)* Working for the Lord. *(Pause.)* I'll receive an inheritance from the Lord. It is the Lord Christ I am serving. Oh, no. *(Looks around, snatches off dirty apron, fixes hair, finds a clean apron, puts it on and exits.)*

Leader: Let's list some people who serve us. *(Possible answers.)* Waitress, maid, appliance repairman, garage mechanic, grocery store checker, nurse, clerk at store, janitor, teachers, lawyers, doctors, and so forth.

1. Do you feel they are servants? Are they your equal?
2. What is expected of a servant according to Luke? *(Possible answers.)* A servant is expected to do his job without praise, has a desire to help others, sensitive, spontaneous, gets involved.
3. Why don't more of us have a servant's heart? *(Too concerned with self, our comfort, what we want to do, others might look down on us.)*
4. Why do we need to check our motives for serving? *(We want to do the right thing for the right reason.)* What are some wrong motives? *(Serve only if we receive recognition or prestige. Choose the church committee we know won't involve anything we don't want to do.)* These Scriptures reveal the proper attitude, Philippians 2:3, 4; Romans 12:10-13.

5. Where do volunteers fit in? How does volunteer work make you feel, not just in the church but in community service? Can you baby-sit for someone so she can do something special, or clean an oven for someone else? Why not surprise someone with an unexpected act of service.

Jesus wants all of us to serve. We may be called upon to do something we don't want to do or feel unqualified to do. The motive behind what we do makes a difference. We need to be willing to serve even if our work goes unnoticed or seems unimportant. We don't always receive public recognition for our services, but we can treasure the joy received from quietly serving others. Our Christian witness in words and deeds may be the only contact some people have with Christ. We can't always see the fruits of our service. Most of our rewards will be received in Heaven. When we serve people, we serve God.

Many of you have heard the story of Albrecht Durer and Franz Knigstein. They were both artists back in the 1490's. Since they were so poor, they decided one would paint and the other would work to support them both. Albrecht painted and promised he would come back and help his friend develop his talent. Franz did hard manual labor which made his hands twisted and stiff so he could no longer hold a paintbrush. One day Albrecht saw Franz praying and today we have the well known work of art called the "Praying Hands." Which man was truly the greatest servant, the man with the shovel or the one with the paintbrush in his hand?

God asked Moses, "What is that in your hand?" "A staff," he replied. God asked Dorcas, "What is that in your hand?" And she replied, "A needle and thread, Lord." What's in your hand?

Taking Action: As you wrote in your journal this month did you see a growth in your attitude? Last month we talked about accessories. As we grow in our Christian life each of our accessories will reflect it. We'll be more compassionate, patient, kind, and loving.

During this month, think about how you serve. In your journal make a list of ways and people you can serve. Be creative and analyze how you are serving. Should it be changed or expanded? Reflect and add to your list ways you might be able to serve. Sometimes we may have to pick and choose. Do something nice for someone that no one else will know about. Make a note in your journal about how happy this makes you feel.

Prayer: Father, we thank You for this time. We pray for the desire to be Your servant. May each of us look at our hands and see what we are holding that we can use for Your glory and honor. We want a willing heart to use what we have. We ask this in Jesus' name, amen.

Song: "Oh Jesus, I Have Promised"

Special

Recognize Mothers

We all know how important a mother's service is. We would like to recognize some of our mothers at this time. *(Use the different categories that pertain to your group. Here are some suggestions you may use. Also the small bucket decorations may be given as prizes for these special mothers.)*
Mother with most children
Mother with most grandchildren and great grandchildren
Youngest and oldest mother
Mothers in different age categories who serve others in unusual ways (community service included)

Memories of Mother

A Reading

The bread dough writhed and rolled in the old metal bread-making bowl as my mother turned the handle on the dough hook. I watched the apple peel curl around my fingers as I helped prepare the apples for the pies Mom would make. Radio stories made the tasks more enjoyable on Saturday baking days.

Mondays were wash days. It was fun to watch the wringer squeeze the soap and water out of the clothes and I longed for the day I could put the clothes through the wringer and slosh them in the double washtubs in the basement. Outside, the still-warm clothes were hung in the sunshine. Tuesday, Mom would iron. She would allow me to iron towels, hankies and pillowcases, but only she ironed Dad's shirts.

Mother's love was shown in these weekly rituals, but she also showed her love by making us Easter outfits and something special at Christmas. Her hands were usually busy crocheting tablecloths or doilies.

Times have changed but mothers haven't. Mothers still fill the kitchen with delightful smells and still prepare Christmas surprises and Easter outfits. Mothers still care more than anyone else about your special hopes and dreams, no matter what your age.

Prayer: Lord, we thank You for our mothers and all they mean to us. Thank You for each mother here. They have a special place in our hearts because they are our mother. We, who are mothers, ask for Your continued wisdom and guidance in our lives no matter the age of our children. We ask this in Jesus' name, amen.

Refreshments: Serve the refreshments during this time of fellowship.

Servant of the King

A servant of the King am I.
Why should I complain?
He sends me out in dusty fields
To seek the lost for Him.

I may not be famous or rich
But serve Him in humble ways.
Help me faithfully do His will
Wherever my path may lead.

Program 10

Changed by Trusting

Name Tag

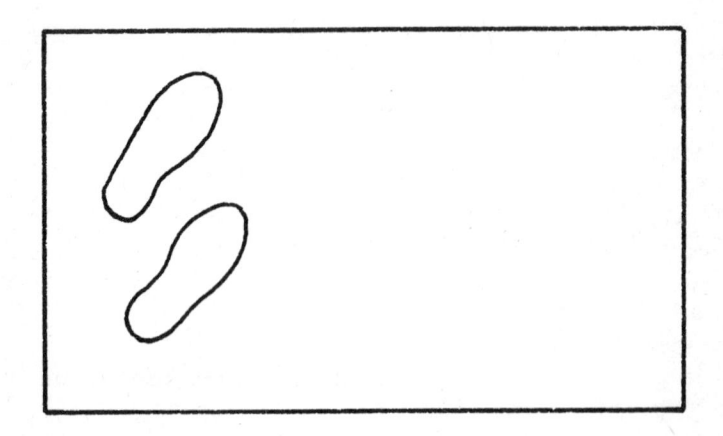

Program Outline

                Song: "He Is Able to Deliver Thee"
              Prayer
          Scripture: Luke 8:40-48
Program Feature: Tape recording from the past.
               Solo: "He Touched Me"
          Discussion
   Taking Action: Write down a step of faith you are going to take.
             Prayer
              Song: "It Is Glory Just to Walk With Him"
     Decorations: Footprints
   Refreshments: Strawberry shortcake

Name Tags may be made using the sample provided here. Introduce your guests and help them feel welcome.

Decorations: Footprints may be placed around the room. Copies of the poem "Footprints" may also be included in the theme.

Refreshments: Strawberry shortcake and beverages

Song: "He Is Able to Deliver Thee"

Prayer: Dear Heavenly Father, at times when circumstances overwhelm us, our faith is very weak. We fear walking through the valleys alone and our footsteps falter. When it is hard to trust, help us to step out in faith knowing You are holding our hand. We want to keep our eyes on You and not on our problems. We ask this in the name of Jesus. Amen.

Scripture: Luke 8:40-48

Program Feature

Leader: Today we are going to listen to a recording of a woman's testimony of faith. I'm sure you will recognize her by her story. She was given a tape recorder to use instead of keeping a written journal.
(A voice from offstage can be used or someone dressed in a long robe could portray the woman in person.)

Her Message

After twelve years of keeping a written journal I decided to try talking into a tape recorder to keep track of my feelings.

Sarah keeps telling me I should go see this man named Jesus. He goes around healing people. From what she has said, I'm convinced He can heal me. After twelve years of chronic bleeding, I'm ready to try anything. I've been to one doctor after another and tried everything. I've even tried the ashes of an ostrich egg wrapped in linen in the summer and cotton in the winter. Jesus is my only hope. I know He can heal me. Sarah told me where I might be able to find Him. I'm going.

This is the day I will be cured and I'm going to take my recorder. It is so small, I'll record my meeting with Jesus. *(Pause.)* If only I can get close. I must get through. I've never seen so many people in the city. *(Pause.)* I feel so weak, why don't I just go home? *(Hopefully.)* But if there is a chance He can heal me, I must go on. He can heal me.

I see His disciples. I've gotten closer. At least no one can move fast with this crowd. When will He stop to heal people? There are so many around Him who need help. They appear to be in worse shape than I am. He won't have time to heal all these people. Others have been helped by His touching them. If He has such power to heal, all I have to do is touch His robe that carries the dust of the road. If I did that, I would be cured. I know it. That wouldn't take time away from all the other desperate people.

There He is. Jesus. Just a little closer. Oh, what right have I to touch even His robe? I'm unclean. So close—yet I dare not. *(Pause.)* I know I can be changed. Dare I? Jesus has His back to me. I'll pretend to stumble. I'll reach out. *(Pause.)* No I shouldn't. Oh, with the press of the crowd I've lost my balance. I did it! I touched His cloak. *(Pause.)* What was that I felt? I know I'm healed. I'll try to fade back into the crowd. Oh no, He stopped. He knows. He wants to know who touched Him. Is He angry? Even the disciples didn't see me.

But Jesus said, "Someone touched me; I know that power has gone out from me" (Luke 8:46). Why don't they go on? I don't want anyone to know. I've been ashamed for so long. Look how I'm shaking, I must confess.

"I did it. I touched your cloak." I couldn't believe the flood of words that poured out of my mouth, after twelve years of being shunned.

Thank you, Jesus. I'll never forget your words to me. "Daughter, your faith has healed you. Go in peace" (Luke 8:48). I'll never be the same. I'm healed. I've been changed by touching His cloak.

Solo or Everyone: "He Touched Me"

Leader: Thank you for the song. Wasn't that an interesting tape? There are several things we can learn from this lady. Twelve years of waiting. Twelve years of being separated from family. She couldn't go to services in a temple or synagogue. She spent hours in doctor's waiting rooms and tried each cure and none of them worked. But she trusted that God could heal her if she touched the robe of Jesus. Let's look at the steps in the woman's faith so that we will be able to step out in faith.

Discussion

She Heard About Jesus (Luke 8:40-48)
 Her faith was stirred. Do we need to stir up our faith and trust in God a little bit? We use faith every day in other areas of our life. We use faith when we flip a light switch. We expect the light to come on. We turn the key in our car and it starts. We accept checks expecting the bank to give us money in return.

1. What can we learn about faith in Hebrews 11:1, 6, 39? *(Answers.)* "Now faith is being sure of what we hope for and certain of what we do not see" (Hebrews 11:1). "And without faith it is impossible to please God, because anyone who comes to him must believe that he exists and that he rewards those who earnestly seek him" (Hebrews 11:6).
 We are told to trust. Trust and unquestioning belief that does not require proof. What did Gideon do in Judges 6:36? He wanted proof and even after the first time wanted more assurance.

She Took Action
 She took action, she left the house. She wanted to be healed secretly.
1. What action did the lady take? She reached out in faith to touch the hem of his cloak.
2. What are some areas we can show our faith by trusting God to take care of them?
    a. We can trust God for our financial needs.
    b. We can trust God for healing us or giving us strength to endure.
    c. We can trust God to work in the hearts of our unsaved spouse or family members.

    d. We can trust God to work things out even when our world falls around us.
3. How much do you trust? Could we have two volunteers?
(At this time you may want to arrange some chairs in a scattered fashion. Blindfold one lady. Another lady will guide her between the chairs. The blindfolded lady must put her trust in the other lady so she won't fall over the chairs. Have the blindfolded lady explain how she felt. Have the other lady tell her feelings of responsibility at being the one to guide.)

Let's look at the next step in the woman's faith. After the lady touched the hem she felt a physical sensation and knew she was healed. Crowds touched Jesus but this was different. He felt power drain from Him.

She Became Involved With Jesus
All the lady wanted was to be healed physically. Jesus didn't want anyone to receive His power without knowing Him personally. He knew she needed a deeper healing and love and forgiveness. That's why He wanted her to come forward. When she confessed she had touched His cloak, Jesus healed her soul and body. She had a new life of peace.

1. How is she typical of us today?
2. Do we feel rejected, left out?
3. Have we carried a trial or problem a long time and live in a seemingly hopeless situation?
4. Are we afraid to try something new?
5. Do we only want the benefits from Jesus but not to know Him personally, to touch and run off?

Taking Action: This month let's find some areas where we can step out in faith. Write in your journal this month ways you can reach out in faith or become more involved with Jesus. In what area do we need to trust God more fully? When we keep up our journal, we can see the footsteps of faith we have taken.

    What did we find out about our serving from our discussion last month? Are we doing what we feel we should be doing? Are we afraid we won't be able to do it? Is this an area where we can be changed by trusting God more fully?

Prayer: Dear Heavenly Father, we want to be like the lady Jesus healed. We want to reach out to You in faith, knowing You will do Your perfect will in our lives. Help us to take one step at a time knowing You are walking hand in hand with us. In His name we pray, amen.

Song: "It Is Glory Just to Walk with Him"

Refreshments: Enjoy this time of physical refreshment as well as spiritual refreshment in fellowship.

Trust

The cupboard's empty, the freezer as well.
No job in the want ads today.
My family has problems, the house is a mess.
The dishes are stacked in the sink.

No one said it would always be easy.
Yet why can't I trust His Word?
God said He would supply my every need.
Help me trust and rejoice in Him.

Program 11

Changed by Obedience

Name Tag

Program Outline

            Song: "The Banner of the Cross"
       Scripture: John 14:23; 15:10
          Prayer
 Program Feature: Parade preparations
      Discussion: Small group discussion
   Taking Action: Is there an area of disobedience in our life?
          Prayer
            Song: "Lead On, O King Eternal"
     Decorations: Clown, parade, balloons
    Refreshments: Ice-cream sundaes

Name Tags may be made using the sample provided here. Be sure to introduce your guests and include them in all the activities.

Decorations: Flags, clowns, balloons, flower decorations in red, white and blue.

Refreshments: Ice-cream sundaes, provide different toppings and allow the ladies to make their own sundaes.

Song: "The Banner of the Cross"

Scripture: John 14:23; 15:10

Prayer: Dear Heavenly Father, from the time we were children we have found it difficult to be obedient. Help us to see during our time together that love and obedience work together. We want to learn how to obey You out of love, not fear, to realize obedience is the working out of love for You. We pray in Jesus' name, amen.

Program Feature

Leader: Our love for God leads us to obedience to Him.
   Our theme today is parades. What goes into a successful parade, not only for the spectators but for the participants? A parade route needs to be planned, permission granted from city officials, and proper permits all need to be taken care of. A grand marshall is chosen as honorary leader.
   We want to think today about how our lives resemble a parade. God has laid out the route in His Word. We are not told each step to take but guidelines are designated. First, we are going to look at a couple of men who certainly had out of the ordinary parade routes.
   We want to all be involved in discovering for ourselves what we can learn from these men. We will break into small groups and each group will go over the Scriptures. Then we will share with each other what each group has learned.
   (Prepare a handout of the questions and Scriptures for each lady. Have the group select a spokesperson to share the group's findings.)

1. Genesis 6:22; Hebrews 11:7
   How difficult do you think it was for Noah to build an ark? It took him 120 years. Put yourself in his shoes or his wife's shoes. What would be the reaction of your family, friends, and neighbors, if you were to do something so unusual? Would you be laughed at and feel rejection? Would you question God about why He is putting you through this?
2. Genesis 22:15-18
   Abraham was willing to sacrifice his only child by Sarah. What message for our lives today can we get from this Bible story?
   a. What do we need to sacrifice?
      Some things are not wrong in themselves, but could we be doing something else of more benefit?
   b. What should our attitude be when we sacrifice? *(obedience and devotion)* "To obey is better than sacrifice" I Samuel 15:22.
      Love and obedience are linked, John 14:23; 15:10.

Leader: *(The group is reassembled. Allow one person from each group to sum up their finding. Then close with these comments.)* We have discovered that the parade route we are to take needs some direction. We may meet up with miles of trials like Noah or be called upon to make sacrifices as Abraham was. If we sacrifice, we want to obey with love.

There are marching units within the parade. Many of them have a drum major with a large baton everyone can see so they can stay in step and follow direction. What would happen if each band member or marcher chose to walk at his own pace. It would not be a very sharp looking unit.

Let's look at a few of the commands Jesus gave us for direction. In John 2:7-11, Jesus told the servants to fill the jars with water. They did. Then he told them to take some wine out and give it to the master of the banquet. They obeyed, the wine was better than the wine previously served.

Luke 5:5 and John 21:6 tell us of different times when the disciples had fished all night and hadn't caught anything; then Jesus told them to let down their nets. Both times the disciples obeyed and their nets were filled.

The most important command Jesus gave is this:

"Love the Lord your God with all your heart and with all your soul and with all your mind and with all your strength. The second is this: Love your neighbor as yourself. There is no commandment greater than these" (Mark 12:30, 31).

(Have some of the ladies look up these Scriptures for other commands and share with the group.)
Love one another, our neighbor, our enemy, Matthew 5:43
Do not worry, Matthew 6:25
Honor your father and mother, Matthew 15:4
Follow me and become fishers of men, Matthew 4:18-20
Love Jesus and obey His commands, John 14:15

A float can be a breath of beauty between marching units. There is much planning and work involved in building a float. A vehicle must be chosen with a large enough motor to handle the weight. The float must be balanced so one end doesn't drag on the street. Forms are built and many times chicken wire used if flowers are to be the main decoration.

What would the float look like if no one read the blueprints or directions? What if each person put the float together as he thought best? You would have chaos.

Let's look at other Scriptures to help us build our float or lives.

Let's use a toy truck as an illustration to help us build a float. As the Scriptures are looked up, lets "build" a float. *(Add the items to the truck as they are mentioned.)*

Truck—Matthew 7:24. The house on the rock, has a firm foundation.

Blocks—James 2:14. Test of faith is obedience. The blocks are the frame to build a platform for a doll to sit on.

Flowers—Romans 8:9. A person is controlled by the Spirit if the Spirit of God lives in him.

Small Doll—Romans 5:5. God's love is poured out on us, we can be motivated by His love for us.

So far in our parade we have talked a little about routes and building floats. There is also a judge's stand where the best floats, marching units, and bands are observed and judged. Sometimes trophies or rewards are given.

Let's read these Scriptures to see some of our rewards.

James 1:25. A person has freedom in obedience.

Matthew 12:50. When we do God's will, we are Christ's sisters.

Isaiah 26:3. We can have perfect peace.

The parade route is long and we may get tired of hearing the bands blaring and the drumbeat becomes a pounding noise to our ear. We may be out of step. The important thing is to be in step with God which puts us out of step with the world. Are we in a position similar to Noah, ridiculed but yet we know we must keep on doing what God asks us to do? Is there something we need to sacrifice as Abraham did?

Taking Action: We want to continue to write in our journals. Is there something we need to do in obedience to God? Make a note of it in your journal. As you read your Bible, look for commands that are given to us to obey, write them in your journal.

Prayer: Dear Heavenly Father, we pray for the desire to obey You in all areas of our lives. We want our actions to always be a result of our love for You. We pray for open hearts and minds when we read Your Word that we may apply those truths to our lives. We thank You for this time and for Your loving care. In Jesus' name, amen.

Song: "Lead On, O King Eternal"

Refreshments: Have fun making your sundaes.

Joy In Obedience

There's no shadow of sin
When we walk with Him.
To obey what He says,
Fears and sorrows flee.
There's joy in obedience
God's smile is our reward.

Program 12

Changed by Praising

Name Tag

Program Outline

Song: "Praise Him! Praise Him!"
Prayer
Scripture: Psalm 145:2
Program Feature: Praise program, worship through Scripture and songs
Prayer
Decorations: Notes of praise
Refreshments: Fruit salad and muffins

Name Tags may be made using the sample provided here. Thank your guests for coming.

Decorations: Make music notes and place around the room.

Refreshments: Fruit salad in a cut-out watermelon bowl, muffins, and beverages

Song: "Praise Him! Praise Him!"

Prayer: Dear Heavenly Father, today we are going to concentrate on learning more about You and how we can worship and praise You in a more meaningful way. Open our hearts and minds to Your message to us and direct our thoughts and words to Your service. We ask this in the name of Your Son, Jesus Christ. Amen.

Scripture: Psalm 145:2

Program Feature

LEADER:
1. What is praise?
   (Possible answers.) Praise is giving approval for a job well done, for someone's attitude, admiration, gratitude and devotion for blessings. It is three cheers for God. Praise is a vocal expression of delight in God. Praise is when we tell about God's goodness, to sing praises and mean the words. Praise is part of worship. Praise is faith in action, to see His hand in everything that happens.

2. Why should we praise God when He knows our thoughts?
   (Possible answers.) We are commanded to praise God. It pleases Him and changes our perspective. The more we focus on God, the more it makes us humble and enlarges our relationship with Him. Praise releases God's power. *(Have ladies look up these Scriptures: Psalm 29:1; Psalm 30:4; Psalm 100:4; Psalm 145:2.)*

3. How can we praise God?
   (Possible answers.) Joyfully. Come with the proper motive of love and adoration. Whenever we tell others about

God's goodness, we are offering the sacrifice of praise. Psalm 111 is a good praise psalm. *(If time allows, read through it together.)* Live in wonder at God's grace and wisdom and our fears will be short-lived.

Let's write a Psalm of Praise. *(Each lady can contribute a line.)* Here is a brief example.
Praise the Lord all ye people.
Thank You for the beauty in the world around us.
Thank You for Your loving care.
Thank You for my friends who helped me through a trying time.

Worship is man's response to God. One of the reasons we worship is to give God glory for who He is and what He has done. We want to be preoccupied with God. To help us focus on worship we are going to do an acrostic of worship. I would like volunteers to look up these Scriptures and tell us what you find. *(Leader assigns the Scriptures. Make a poster for each letter to spell the word WORSHIP.)* After we share each group of Scriptures we will sing a song of praise.

W onder of our Creator and His creation
Revelation 4:11; Psalm 104:1, 24; Psalm 95:6, 7
Song: "For the Beauty of the Earth" (one verse)

O mnipresent
Psalm 139:7-10; Matthew 18:20; 1 Timothy 1:17
Song: "Immortal, Invisible, God Only Wise"

R uler
2 Chronicles 20:6; Psalm 93:1, 2; 1 Timothy 6:15-17
Song: "O Worship the King" (one verse)

S hepherd
Isaiah 40:11; John 10:14-16
Song: "Guide Me, O Thou Great Jehovah"

H oly
Psalm 99:9; Isaiah 6:3; Exodus 15:11
Song: "Holy, Holy, Holy" (one verse)

I mmutable
    Psalm 102:27; James 1:17; Hebrews 13:8
    Song: "Jesus Is the Sweetest Name I Know"

P erfection
    Psalm 18:30, Deuteronomy 32:4; Matthew 5:48
    Song: "How Great Thou Art!" *(one verse)*

Prayer: Dear Lord, we are humbled by the beauty of Your creation and awed by the wonder of You. May we leave here wanting to make praise and worship a part of our daily walk with You. Enlarge our view of Your glory and help us to remember to praise You. We ask in Jesus' name, amen.

Refreshments: Enjoy the food and fellowship.

Praise

At times I shout "Hallelujah"
    Or "Praise the Lord."
At times I whisper and
    God and I join hearts.

Give this handout as a reminder of the changes that have taken place in our lives during the past year. Use it as a reminder to thank God for His answer to your prayer "Lord, change me."

    CHANGE ME (Ruth 1)
    CHANGED BY STORMS (Mark 4:35-41)
    CHANGED BY THANKING (1 Thessalonians 5:18)
    CHANGED BY GOD'S GIFT (Luke 2:1-20)
    CHANGED BY BIBLE STUDY (2 Timothy 3:16)
    CHANGED BY LOVE (1 John 3:7-24)
    CHANGED BY PRAYER (1 Chronicles 29:10-13)
    CHANGED APPEARANCE (Colossians 3:12-14)
    CHANGED BY SERVING (Luke 17:7-10)
    CHANGED BY TRUSTING (Luke 8:40-48)
    CHANGED BY OBEDIENCE (John 14:23; 15:10)
    CHANGED BY PRAISING (Psalm 145:2)